Frontpiece. Tombstone friends, friendly enemies? This charcoal drawing by R. Hupp was taken from a photograph that appeared in the November, 1972 American West magazine and allegedly shows, from L to R, standing: Doc Holliday, Tom McLowry, Ike Clanton, Morgan Earp and Billy Clanton. Seated: Luke Short and Wyatt Earp. Tom McLowry, with Doc Holliday's arm over his shoulder was killed at the gunfight along with Billy Clanton. George Hart, owner of the photograph, and the American West magazine staff believe the photo is authentic. Collection of the authors.

WYATT EARP

The Missing Years

SAN DIEGO
In the 1880s

First edition, first printing
January, 1998
3000 copies

First edition, second printing
August, 2003
2000 copies

Published by

Gaslamp Books/Museum
413 Market Street
San Diego, California, 92101
Telephone (619) 237-1492
Fax (619) 237-5537
E-Mail gaslampbooks@earthlink.net

*This book is dedicated to two special women:
Lenora, wife and mother;
and in loving memory of Hazel Marie Cilch.*

FOREWARD

The Ken Cilch's book on Wyatt Earp fills a void in the historical studies of the West's most famous lawman.

Earp's career, bringing a semblance of law and order to the cattle drive towns of Ellsworth, Wichita and Dodge City, Kansas is legendary, as is the gunfight at the OK Corral in Tombstone, and Earp's later life in Hollywood of the 1920s where his pals (later pallbearers) included movie cowboy Tom Mix and William S. Hart, is well known.

But the period of Wyatt Earp's life from 1885 until the end of the century, when Earp largely resided in (and roamed out from) San Diego, California - has been largely ignored, until now. In this Southwest Border town, Wyatt owned bars, organized South-of-the-Border gambling, and least known of all (but most central to all of his long life), prospected and mined. He owned mining claims and worked all over the West, from the mountains east of San Diego, to the Mohave south of Needles, to Idaho and the Corue d'Alene, through the Colorado Rockies and even around Tombstone. Like thousands of others, he was also lured to the Yukon gold rush.

Wherever he went, Wyatt Earp generated the following of men of adventure who instinctively seek out fearlessness; and he created adventures, as inevitably as a cattle drive creates dust.

Ken Cilch is a lawman himself. A retired parole officer, he is a "man of the badge," an outdoorsman, miner and businessman, and a writer. His prose reminds one of Heinrich Herrer's fine straightforwardness in his 1953 book, *Seven Years in Tibet*, (recently made into a Brad Pitt movie). In his forward, Herrer protests his lack of experience as a writer, concluding... I shall content myself with the unadorned facts."

Cilch has uncovered significant new Earp sources, including many period newspaper articles, and salient among these are articles written by Clara S. Brown, the San Diego Union's 1880s "stringer reporter" for Arizona, who lived in Tombstone at the time of the OK Corral gunfight.

The lore of the West has been expanded by the Cilch's new work. Western buffs will enjoy the ride!

Robert C. Coates
Judge of the Municipal Court
San Diego, California
October 21, 1997

TABLE OF CONTENTS

ILLUSTRATIONS

Frontcover. Photograph of an oil painting of youthful Wyatt Earp, artist and date unknown. Courtesy San Diego Historical Society, Photo Collection.

Frontpiece. Tombstone friends, friendly enemies?

Page

PREFACE

Who was Wyatt Earp? Wyatt Earp was a remarkable man. He led a remarkable life. In the eyes of the public, he surpasses other great legendary figures of the Western frontier, such as Buffalo Bill, Wild Bill Hickok, Billy the Kid and General George Custer.

From 1875 to 1908, Wyatt and his wife, Josephine Marcus Earp, were first hand witnesses to and active participants in the development of the Western frontier. After Tombstone, where they met, the Earps lived together for forty-seven years. Their lives were colorful and adventurous. During this span they visited every major mining discovery in North America. We are not aware of any other individual of Wyatt's status who visited all of the gold and silver strikes including Deadwood, South Dakota; Coeur d' Alene, Idaho; Tombstone, Arizona; the Klondike Goldrush; and Tonopah, Goldfield, Nevada as well as many other minor gold discoveries.

Wyatt's other activities included being part of his father's wagon train that traveled from Pella, Iowa to California in the 1860's. He drove freight wagons and stagecoaches, rode shotgun on stages carrying gold bullion, hunted buffalo, refereed boxing matches, was involved in professional gambling and horse racing, operated saloons, and as a businessman, invested in real estate and mining properties. However, his best known activity was as a law enforcement officer. His exploits in Kansas, Ellsworth, Wichita and Dodge City are legendary. His participation in the fabled shootout at Tombstone's OK Corral is known worldwide.

He rubbed shoulders with the "greats" of this western era. While hunting buffalo he met Buffalo Bill and Bat Masterson. At Dodge City, he knew most of the famous Texas cattle owners and their trail bosses, prominent badmen and gunfighters and, of course, legendary lawmen. Here he became lifelong friends with Doc Holliday, considered by many to be the most dangerous man in the West.

Later in life he and Josie associated with multi-millionaire Lucky Baldwin, legendary Death Valley Scotty, fight promoter Tex Rickard, poet Robert Service, authors Jack London and Rex Beach, heavyweight champion Jack Dempsey and his colorful manager, Doc Kearns. In the Yukon, on their way to Dawson City, they were snowed in for an entire winter with scant provisions and lodging. In the early days of the movie industry, he made close friends of actors William S. Hart, Tom Mix, and director John Ford.

There is little doubt that Wyatt's activities as a law enforcement officer have been exaggerated. Most western heroes have been made larger then life, mostly the result of zealous writers. Moreover, some contend that Wyatt and his brothers were crooks and whoremongers. There is no evidence that this is true. But, in the course of owning and operating saloons and gambling halls, they undoubtedly were involved in hiring dance hall girls, many of whom were prostitutes. In those days, owners of saloons and the like were respected members of their communities. You cannot judge nine-teenth century pioneer people and their practices and morals by our present day standards.

The authors feel that Wyatt and his brothers Virgil and Morgan, along with friend Bat Masterson, stand as symbols of all great West-ern lawmen. Their courage, decency, strength, level-headedness, and sense of responsibility were qualities which helped tame the wild frontier. However, this assessment of the Earps and Bat Masterson is challenged by a number of Western writers.

When we opened our used and rare book store in the Gaslamp Quarter in 1992, we began to research this old area. Neither of us were historians in the academic sense but were fascinated by west-ern history and had developed an extensive library on the subject. We immediately began to hear stories of the roaring 1880s in down-town San Diego and, in particular, Wyatt Earp's presence. Similar to the east coast where every inn claimed that "Washington slept here," every old hotel in San Diego claimed that "Wyatt slept here."

We gradually became amateur Earp historians. It soon became clear to us that little was known of Wyatt's activities in San Diego. For this reason, this interval is described by the authors as the "missing years". In time, we uncovered oral histories and newspaper articles that described Wyatt's activities during this colorful era. We located sites where he lived and operated businesses. These sites are shown in a walking tour map of San Diego's "Red Light district of the 1880s," which is included in the book. The Gaslamp Quarter, formerly known as the Stingaree District, is now designated as a historic area and is noted for its Victorian architecture.

Wyatt and Josie were both full-time and part-time residents of San Diego from about 1885 to the mid 1890s. They enjoyed San Diego and made a lot of money in the boom years of 1886-88. Wyatt was viewed as a respected businessman and gambler.

While Wyatt gained his reputation in Kansas cow towns such as Dodge City and at the OK Corral in Tombstone, Arizona Territory, this span of time covered only three or four years. For most of the remainder of his long life he lived in Southern California, either in San Diego, San Bernardino, Los Angeles or in the desert near Earp, California.

We hope that our efforts will be useful to the field of Earp literature and interesting to the reader.

ACKNOWLEDGEMENTS

The authors wish to acknowledge the assistance of the following people for their help in this endeavor: First to my good friend, the late Nick Johnson for his editing skills and expertise with the computer. Nick edited the first draft of this effort just days before his death. His advice and guidance are highly esteemed and appreciated. He contributed much. He will be missed.

Herb Cilch and his son John Cilch for major research assistance at both the San Diego Public Library and visiting Wyatt's old claims near Earp, California; Jennifer Cilch for research efforts at the Bancroft Library at Berkeley and locating Wyatt and Josie's graves at Colma, California; Don Rogers for valuable research at the San Diego Public Library and securing material from Wyatt's hometown at Pella, Iowa; Don Cilch for his awesome memory in recalling our visit to Wyatt's mine over fifty years ago; old friend Mike Sullivan for research at the Needles, California newspapers and help in relocating Wyatt's mine; friend Kathy Flanigan, researcher extraordinare, who continues to find gems of Earp memorabilia; Judge Robert C. Coates, our mining partner, for valuable insights and encouragement; G. S Lamprey for his financial planning and motivational expertise; Lauren Cilch, John C. (Jack) Roberts and Lincoln W. Higgie for diligent editing and proof reading; Jerry Sullivan for his photographs of Wyatt's mine, and Charles Dyer for his editing and suggestions on format. Our thanks also to Downtown Sam for his knowledge of the Stingaree District and friends Hugo Fisher and Don Reeves for their historical expertise. Thanks to free lance writer Paul R. Maracin who meticulously edited the final draft and made valuable suggestions concerning format and content. And finally to Jeanene "Chili" Cilch, who, when we were floundering with the first edition, took charge and brought it to fruition.

Special thanks to Barbara Kousens for her computer expertise and dedication to the project, and to her and Bill Burns for the final edit.

For further reading about the Wyatt Earp legend, Stuart Lake's *Wyatt Earp, Frontier Marshal,* is a must. This is the book that started the Earp legend. It was published two years after Wyatt's death and became a national best seller. It is extraordinarily well written. Lake was the only biographer to interview Wyatt.

Glen Boyer, editor of Josie Earp's book, *I Married Wyatt Earp,* and his new book, *Vendetta,* make interesting reading. Boyer is one of the foremost authorities on the Earp legend.

Richard E. Erwin, author of *The Truth About Wyatt Earp,* presents a very interesting and balanced account of the controversy concerning the "Wyatt Earp character" issue. Was Wyatt a saint or sinner?

Much of the material in this narrative is based on these publications.

We must also thank the crew of the San Diego Historical Society for their friendliness and alerting the authors to their Oral History Program which contained interviews with San Diego Pioneers. This was an invaluable source of Earp material and information on San Diego of the 1880s.

A word of thanks to the Arizona Historical Society at Tucson for their permission to publish their photographs of Wyatt in his later years. Some of these photographs were donated to their society in recent years by Earp heirs and have never, to my knowledge, been seen by the public.

Our heartfelt thanks to all.

Ken Cilch, Sr.
Ken Cilch, Jr.
San Diego, California

Chapter One

EARLY HISTORY

Wyatt Berry Stapp Earp was born on March 19, 1848 at Monmouth, Illinois. His parents, Nicholas Earp and Victoria Ann Cooksley, were married in 1840. Wyatt had five brothers and one sister. Half brother Newton, James and Virgil were older and Morgan, Warren and sister Adelia were younger. Wyatt was named after his father's commanding officer in the Mexican War of 1847.

In about 1850, Nicholas Earp moved his family to Pella, Iowa, a Dutch community where he farmed and was appointed Justice of the Peace. The family remained in this community off and on for sixteen years. The family home is now a museum.

An interesting and touching story of these early years concerns Wyatt's brother Virgil. At age seventeen, Virgil ran off and married a young Pella lass by the name of Ellen Rysdam and she bore him a baby daughter, Nellie Jane. This did not sit well with the girls relatives and Virgil was never accepted into her family. As a result, Virgil enlisted in the Union Army and remained until the Civil War ended in 1865. In the meantime, the girl's family spread the word that Virgil had been killed in action and the family moved to the Oregon Territory where Ellen later remarried. Many years later, the daughter, Nellie Jane, read about her father and made contact with him after her mother's death. When Virgil died in 1905, he was buried in Portland, Oregon beside his first wife. The arrangements were made by the daughter. 1

In 1863, the father, filled with wanderlust, organized a wagon train to California. After a seven month trek, the family arrived in the San Bernardino-Colton area of Southern California. Enroute, sixteen year old Wyatt supplied the wagon train with fresh meat . He was an excellent shot. Wyatt left Iowa a boy and arrived in California a man. Nicholas returned to the Midwest several years

Photographs of Wyatt as a youth are rare. This photograph of an oil painting by L. McCarty is dated 1956. The artist indicates what Wyatt may have looked like in 1881. Courtesy San Diego Historical Society, Photo Collection.

later. He led another wagon train west and eventually settled for good at Colton in Southern California, where he became a businessman and was appointed as Justice of the Peace.

At age seventeen Wyatt secured employment driving wagons from San Bernardino to Los Angeles and later from Colton to Salt Lake City. This was a distance of seven hundred miles over some of the most rugged terrain in the west and through hostile Indian country. Wyatt was a mature and courageous teenager.

In 1868 Wyatt returned to Monmouth, Ill. to visit his grandfather, Walter Earp. While there, he met and married Urilla Southerland, who may have died in childbirth. After her death and filled with grief, he spent several years at odd jobs ending up in Kansas. Here he met and established a lifetime friendship with Bat Masterson. He and Bat made good money hunting buffalo. Buffalo hides were in great demand, but the meat was left to rot. They also witnessed the depletion of the great buffalo herds which led to the demise of the Plains Indians. These Indians depended on the buffalo for food and the hides for clothing. Wyatt was quoted as stating that he and Bat Masterson once observed at least one million buffalo in one herd.2   In the ten year interval of the 1870s, millions of buffalo werc slaughtered. There is some feeling that the Federal Government encouraged this slaughter of the buffalo in order to deprive the Plains Indians of their main source of food and clothing. It also opened up the area for farming, which would not have been possible with millions of buffalo migrating north and south.

According to John Myers, in his book *Doc Holliday,* Wyatt was a Marshal in Ellsworth, Kansas in 1874.3 It was later, however, at Wichita, Kansas, where Wyatt began to establish his reputation as one of the premier lawman of the west. He was appointed to the Wichita Police Force in 1875 and later that year appointed a deputy marshal.

Wichita in 1874 was passing its peak as a wild and woolly

cowtown and terminus of the famous Chisholm Trail. In its heyday, Wichita was a wild and wicked town and a challenge for local law enforcement. Keeping the boisterous cowhands under control took courage and fortitude. This established Wyatt's reputation as a fearless and determined lawman.

In 1876, because of his reputation, Wyatt was invited to visit Dodge City, Kansas where he subsequently was appointed deputy marshal. His exploits in Dodge City further enhanced his reputation as the most outstanding lawman of his time. While some of his exploits in Dodge City were exaggerated by many reporters of the time, there is no doubt that he and his fellow marshals such as Bat Masterson, kept the city under control.

At this time Dodge City was recognized as the wildest of frontier towns. The population consisted of U.S. Army cavalrymen from Fort Dodge, railroad workers, buffalo hunters, mule-skinners, gamblers, dancehall girls and Texas cowhands who came with a grudge against northerners. Many of these cowhands were either confederate veterans or Southern sympathizers. This was an explosive mix. The cowboys, fresh from the trail, would swagger through town, riding their horses into saloons, firing their revolvers at will. It was a point of pride that they would take over the town and they did this until the arrival of Wyatt Earp. The first marshal, Billy Brooks, killed or wounded fifteen men before being run out of town. This became routine practice for his law enforcement successors. The city fathers hired some of the toughest gun hands in the West but they all were either killed or also chased out of town. When Wyatt arrived the boothill cemetery contained seventy or eighty men who had met violent deaths. How Wyatt and his fellow lawmen tamed this town is a matter of legend.

Bat Masterson stated many times that Wyatt Earp was the fastest man with a gun that he had ever seen. His marksmanship was also phenomenal. Despite his prowess with a gun, he apparently never killed a man while at Dodge City. However, he did crack many a cowboy's skull with the barrel of his gun or knocked them out with his fists. As a youth he had boxed exhibition matches and was good with his fists. The businessmen liked this approach to law enforcement as a dead cowboy was a non-paying customer.

What did Wyatt look like? Wyatt was just a shade over six feet in height, weighed about 160 pounds and had russet blond hair that was parted and swept back over his head. A long mustache highlighted his face. He had deep-set blue eyes and was considered handsome by many women.

However, his most pronounced attributes were his lack of fear, his high degree of confidence in himself and his strength of character. Many old timers have related how Wyatt could influence, sometimes almost mystically, friends and foes alike. He enjoyed the utmost respect of his family and friends and many of his enemies.

In 1876, gold was discovered at Deadwood City, South Dakota in the Black Hills. In this same year, the population of Dodge City was declining and the town was becoming quiet. Wyatt, his brothers and Bat Masterson then headed for the new goldfields. In a business sense this move did not prove profitable for the Earp faction.

Later in the same year Wyatt returned to Dodge City as marshal. It was during this interval that Wyatt and Doc Holliday became lifelong friends. It is reported that Doc Holliday saved Wyatt's life twice in the same evening. While the rest of Dodge City's law enforcement officials were out on a posse hunting down renegade Indians a large group of drunken cowboys decided to shoot up the town. Wyatt heard gunshots and when he went to investigate, two cowboys stepped out of the shadows with their guns drawn. They got the drop on Wyatt and marched him at gun point to where twenty or thirty cowboys had gathered. They taunted Wyatt to draw. Wyatt later stated that he thought his time had come. However, Doc Holliday overheard the commotion and came out of a nearby saloon with gun in each hand. He challenged the cowboys to fight or back off. This gave Wyatt time to draw his own gun and the two faced the drunken mob. Wyatt is alleged to have quietly spoken to two older, noted cattlemen who were in front of the mob. "If you kill me, I'm going to take you two with me." With that, the two older cattlemen turned their backs and moved away, stating, "Lets go boys, there will always be another day." As the cowboys moved away, one drunk cowboy drew his gun and aimed at Wyatt. Before the cowboy could get off a shot, Doc shot him in the arm.

Why Doc came to Wyatt's rescue that evening is unknown. Bat Masterson tried to explain it by stating on more then one occasion that Wyatt had about him an unusual quality that drew men to him and that he also had the ability to make lifelong friends. Bat was another friend who felt Wyatt was without fear. In any event, Wyatt and Doc remained good friends throughout their lives.

Virgil Earp's resting place in Portland, Oregon. He is buried next to his first wife, Ellen. Collection of authors.

This revealing photo of Josie Earp was probably taken in Tombstone and indicates she may have been a dance hall girl or such. Few women posed this way in the 1880s. Author Glenn G. Boyer used this same photograph on the cover of Josie's biography which he edited, and entitled *I Married Wyatt Earp*. Recently, however, some have questioned the photograph's authenticity. Collection of the authors.

Chapter Two
THE EARPS AT TOMBSTONE

In 1879, Wyatt, his brothers and their wives set out for the new silver mining town of Tombstone, to establish a stageline and invest in business opportunities. They traveled by wagon and arrived in Tombstone in November. Upon finding that two stage coach lines were already in operation, Wyatt accepted an appointment as under sheriff and brother Morgan hired on to the police department. The brothers eventually secured the gambling concession at several saloons including the famous Oriental. They invested also in several mining properties which, unfortunately, did not pan out.

Few people are aware that Wyatt's problems in Tombstone were related to partisan politics. He and his brothers, Virgil and Morgan, were active Republican lawmen in a Democratically controlled town. Tombstone's Democratic sheriff, Johnny Behan, was a typically crooked politician some say and the Earp brothers' worst enemy. He came to hate Wyatt, initially, because his live-in girlfriend, Josie Marcus, took a shine to Wyatt and eventually moved out on Johnny and in with Wyatt. This is a little known fact.

A few words are due Josephine Marcus Earp who by all accounts was a remarkable woman. Josie, as she was known, was born into a well-to-do Jewish family of merchants in San Francisco. In her book, *I Married Wyatt Earp*, she indicates that she ran away from home at seventeen years of age and toured the western mining camps with a theatrical group performing various Gilbert and Sullivan operettas.4 When the troupe hit Tombstone, she met and fell for Johnny Behan, the local sheriff and moved in with him. Johnny refused to marry her and may have made her work as a dance hall girl. This may account for the almost totally nude photo of her that was first seen in San Francisco. Boyer featured this photo on the front cover of her book but darkened sections of the photo to hide the nudity The author recently secured a clear copy of this photo taken directly from a glass negative. Not many women posed nude in the 1880s. [No wonder Josie was vague when discussing these years.] However, the authenticity of this photograph is questioned in some circles.

Some authors have criticized Wyatt for taking up with Josie and leaving Mattie Blaylock, his common law wife. Wyatt and Mattie hooked up in Dodge City where she was thought to be a dance hall girl. Wyatt brought her with him to Tombstone. Although they lived together, there is no record that they were ever married. Richard E. Erwin, in his book, *The Truth About Wyatt Earp*, claims that Mattie accompanied the Earp clan when they left Tombstone for the family home at Colton, California.5 This could be true, but does not seem logical, since Josie was with this group. In her later years, Josie would not allow anyone to mention Mattie's name. Josie was insanely possessive of Wyatt. Some years later, Mattie is alleged to have died from a broken heart and a drug overdose in some small western town.

The outlaw element was responsible for a reign of terror, in and around Tombstone. When the Earps arrived in Tombstone, they assumed a variety of law enforcement roles. This threw a monkey wrench into the outlaw's operations and plans. Doc Holliday, Wyatt's friend from Dodge City, joined the Earp faction and backed their play. Their honest law enforcement efforts enraged the cowboys and their cohort, Sheriff Johnny Behan and they swore revenge.

John Clum, editor of the *Tombstone Epitaph*, the Republican newspaper, and most other businessmen backed the Earp faction. By the way, this newspaper continues to be published today. Clum was a lifelong friend of Wyatt's and a pall bearer at his funeral. He was a giant of a man in his own right. Prior to coming to Tombstone, he was Indian agent for the Apache Nation and dealt directly with Geronimo and other Apache chiefs. He resigned this position in disgust over the way the government treated the Indians. He was also the first mayor of Tombstone. He organized the Tombstone vigilantes, and survived a serious attempt on his life by outlaws as well. Later in life he established the postal system in Alaska.

On October 26, 1881 the buildup of hostilities between the two factions culminated in the most famous and talked about gunfight in the annals of western folklore, the Gun Battle at the O K Corral. On this date, the Earp brothers and Doc Holliday faced cowboys Frank and Thomas McLowry with Ike and Billy Clanton. As a result, Billy Clanton and the McLowry brothers were killed. Ike Clanton ran away. Virgil and Morgan Earp as well as Doc Holliday were slightly wounded. Wyatt escaped without injury.

The San Diego Union newspaper covered the events in Tombstone by telegraphic dispatches and by apparently utilizing a woman reporter. During this turbulent period, Clara S. Brown sent a series of dispatches to the *San Diego Union* which were termed, *Letters From Tombstone.*6 Her letter, as it was published in the newspaper follows, unedited:

"Tombstone, Arizona Territory, October 29, 1881, Editor, *Union*; Since my last writing, much has occurred, in this vicinity to interest the public mind.

But your telegraphic reports from Tombstone are now so comprehensive that its seems but a repetition for me to write concerning the same events and I can only treat of some minor details which have not been mentioned.

Following the Indian scare, stage robbery and important mining suits we have been shocked by the most tragic and bloody occurrence which has transpired in the history of the camp. As you have probably learned the particulars by telegraph, I will pass lightly over the events of that memorable day.

The inmates of every house in town were greatly startled by the sudden report of firearms about 3 P.M., discharged with such lightning-like rapidity that it could only be compared to the explosion of a bunch of firecrackers: and the aspect of affairs grew more portentous when, a few minutes later, the whistles of the steam hoisting works sounded shrill alarm. The cowboys cried out, thinking that a party of those desperadoes were taking the town. The Indians were the most excitable. Then, after it was learned that a fight had been engaged in between Marshal Earp, his two brothers, a deputy and four cowboys, resulting in the death of three of the latter and the wounding of three of the former, speculation as to the cause of the affair ran riot. In the middle of this, when the scene upon the streets was one of great excitement, the whistle again sounded and directly, well armed citizens appeared from all quarters, prepared for any emergency.

This revealed what was not before known, the existence of a vigilante committee, composed of law abiding citizens, who organized with determination of upholding right and combatting wrong and who agreed upon a signal of action (whistles) from the mines. Their services were not needed, however on this occasion no further trouble ensued.

A guard of ten men was placed around the jail and extra policemen brought into service for the night.

Three young men, one only nineteen and the oldest twenty-nine were handsomely laid out and buried on the following day in the most imposing manner possible in this part of the country. A stranger viewing the cortege, which was the largest ever seen in Tombstone would have thought that some person esteemed by the entire camp was being conveyed to his final resting place. The Tombstone band headed the long line of carriages, footmen and horsemen. The two McLowry brothers were interred in the same grave." End of news dispatch.

This dispatch has never before been reported in book form and attempts to identify Clara S. Brown have been unsuccessful. That a woman, apparently from San Diego, was almost an eye witness to the gunfight at the OK Corral and served as a news correspondent for a newspaper in the 1880s was a milestone for the time.

As expected, Sheriff Behan issued warrants for Holliday and the Earps, arrested them and charged them with murder. This is the reason that the vigilantes surrounded the jail, to protect the Earps and Doc Holliday. The trial lasted thirty days before Judge Wells Spicer. The verdict read: "the defendants were fully justified in committing these homicides; that it was a necessary act done in the discharge of official duty." This verdict was received with outrage by the cowboys. The life of the judge was threatened and an attempt was made to murder John Clum, the editor of the *Tombstone Epitaph.*

Worse was to come. Within days, the Earps, Judge Wells Spicer and John Clum received death threats through the mail. On December 14, 1881 a stage coach in which John Clum was riding was fired upon by unknown assailants. He leaped from the stage in the darkness and walked to safety. In less than thirty days, Virgil Earp, U.S. Deputy Marshal was ambushed, shot in the arm and crippled for life. The assailants were not found.

Virgil Earp was a fine lawman in his own right. In his book, *Virgil Earp Western Peace Officer*, Don Chaput states, "Virgil was never the subject of a cult or the stuff of legends."[7] However, he carved out a fine career in law enforcement from Prescott and Tombstone, Arizona Territory, Colton,California and Tonopah, Nevada.

Three months later, Morgan Earp was shot and killed while shooting pool with Wyatt and friends. Again, the assailants were not found.

Again another dispatch from Clara S. Brown that appeared in the *San Diego Union* under the byline, *Letter From Tombstone*:

> "The Murder of Morgan Earp, Tombstone, March 18, 1881.[8] Morgan Earp, one of the principles in the shooting which occurred on the 28th of last November in which Frederick and Tom McLowrey and Billy Clanton were killed, was shot at ten minutes of eleven tonight while playing billiards in Campbell and Hatch's saloon.
>
> "Two shots were fired through a glass door. The fatal shot hit him in the abdomen, passing through the body and shattering the spinal column. He died at twelve o'clock midnight. The other shot was aimed at his brother Wyatt, US Deputy Marshal, who was sitting on the other side of the room, the ball passing over his head and lodging in the wall. There is no clue to the assassins. The evidence shows that two or more were engaged in the assassination." This ends the news dispatch.
>
> Another dispatch from Clara: " Earp assassination, March 20, 1882, Tombstone."[9] " The coroners jury found that Morgan Earp was killed

by Stillwell and others. The Sheriff was at the head of a gang of cowboys, hunting the Earps. A nice community.

The coroners jury found that Morgan Earp came to his death at the hands of Frank Stilwell, (who was killed the next day in Tucson). Accomplices were Pete Spencer, one of his friends, and two half-breed indians. Pete Spencer's wife exposed the plot. A sheriff's posse consisting of twenty men, mostly cowboys left this morning for the Dragoon mountains where the Earps are expected to be present. The sheriff made a weak attempt to arrest them at the Cosmopolitan Hotel before they left, but Wyatt Earp told him he didn't want to see him, that he had seen him once too often and the Earp's party mounted their horses and rode away. There is a very uneasy feeling among the cowboy element as the Earps are rendered desperate by the attempted assassination of Virgil Earp and cold-blooded murder of Morgan Earp." End of news dispatch.

Morgan's body, accompanied by the entire Earp clan, was shipped to the family home at Colton, California for burial. Enroute, the train was stopped at Tucson where Wyatt learned that another ambush was imminent. He and Doc Holliday stepped off the train and several minutes later shots were heard. Frank Stilwell, a cowboy with an unsavory reputation and by then a suspect in the killing of Morgan, was found the next morning lying on the railroad tracks shot dead.

Two dispatches from Clara regarding these incidents were entitled *A Bloody Sequel, the Assassination of Morgan Earp and The Assassination of Frank Stilwell in Tucson.*

"Tucson, Arizona Territory, March 20, 1882.[10] Two of the Earp brothers and Doc Holliday arrived here tonight from Tombstone and Virgil Earp passed on to Colton with the remains of his brother Morgan who was assassinated Saturday night in Tombstone. A body of fifteen armed men accompanied the brothers from Tombstone and there is no danger of them being molested."

A Cowardly and Mysterious Assassination.11 Tucson, March 21, 1882. This morning at daylight, the trackman at the Southern Pacific Railroad Depot found the body of Frank Stilwell about 100 yards north of Porter Hotel at the side of the track riddled with bullets. Circumstances of the case as far as known are as follows: Stilwell arrived here on Sunday to appear before the grand jury on a charge of stage robbery near Bishop last November. He was making bond for his appearance. Last night when the west bound passenger train arrived, it brought the remains of Morgan Earp, who had been killed on Saturday night at Tombstone and his three brothers accompanied by Sherman McMasters, Doc Holliday and a man known as Johnson, all heavily armed with shotguns and revolvers. A few minutes before the train started, Stilwell and Ike Clanton, brother of the Clanton who was killed at Tombstone by the Earps went to the train to meet a man by the name of McDowell who was to come in as a witness before the grand jury. On their arrival at the depot they saw the Earp party walking on the platform. Stilwell urged Ike Clanton to leave at once saying that they wanted to kill him. Clanton left a few minutes later. Stilwell was seen walking down the track in the direction of where his body was found. Some of the armed men who were on the platform soon followed. One was described as a slender, light complexioned man wearing a light hat. Just as the train was leaving, six shots were heard in the locality of the assassination but attracted no particular attention and nothing was known of the tragedy until this morning when the body was discovered. Six shots went into his body, four rifle balls and two loads of buckshot. Both legs were shot through and there was a charge of buckshot in his left thigh and a charge through his breast which must have been delivered at close range as his coat had powder burns and there were six buckshot holes within a radius of three inches. Stilwell had had a pistol on his person which was taken. He must have been taken unawares, as he was desperate in a fight and a quick shot. His watch was taken in a hurry, of which a part of the chain was left. There is much excitement here concerning the assassination and many speculations are rife. Some say he was decoyed to the spot where he fell as he possessed strong evidence against certain stage robbers. Others think he was trying to get away from the Earp party and was overtaken, while it is thought by some that he went down the track to shoot one or more of the Earp party as the train was moving out.

The killing is thought to have been done by four of the party who accompanied the Earps here as the four men who followed the deceased down the track were not seen again. This morning at 1:00 A.M., as the eastbound freight train approached the Papago Mine, a few miles north of here, it was flagged down and four armed men got on the train.

The deceased was twenty-seven years of age and was a native of Texas. He was a brother to the famous Texas scout Jack Stilwell. He had been in Arizona four years and was a teamster for a time and lately operated a stable at Charleston and was an ex-deputy sheriff at Colton County. Yesterday, Ike Clanton received several dispatches from Tombstone warning him to look out, that a party was coming down to put him out of the way, which put him on his guard. The authorities here are determined to get to the bottom of this matter and if the parties are apprehended there will be no brief examination but a trial on the merits and the guilty parties, whoever they may be will suffer the penalty of the law." End of news dispatch.

Another dispatch from Clara S. Brown regarding this incident, dated March 23, 1882, Tombstone.[12]

"Attempt to arrest the Earp parties on their return to Tombstone-more bloodshed. The Earp party arrived in Tombstone at 1:00 PM and went to the Cosmopolitan Hotel and stayed there until 7:00 PM this evening until Sheriff Behan went to arrest them. After they drew their guns on Sheriff Behan, they mounted their horses and left for the hills.

The feeling here in Tucson in regard to the assassination of Stilwell is growing more intense hourly. The deceased was here in response to a subpoena from the court. It is now generally believed that the bandits came down from Tombstone for the purpose of seeing Ike Clanton who has been here for two weeks. Today after the hearing, a warrant was placed in the hand for the arrest of the Earp party, Holliday, McMasters and others of the implicated parties. Learning that they had returned to and arrived at Tombstone this afternoon, Sheriff Paul telegraphed Sheriff Behan of Cochise County at Tombstone to arrest the parties. Tonight, Sheriff Behan telegraphed Sheriff Paul that he attempted to make the arrest and was forcibly resisted by the party and a posse of their friends and he asked for assistance as the Earp party fled to the hills. Sheriff Paul left tonight on a special for Tombstone to make the arrest. There is no doubt that he will take them, but bloodshed is expected." End of news dispatch.

This was the last straw. Wyatt led the Earp faction back to Tombstone while their women continued on to the parent's home in Colton, California. Soon an informer supplied the names of the other assailants. Wyatt then formed a vigilante posse to hunt down the other killers of his brother. In rapid succession, Indian Charley was shot down and killed by the posse and Curley Bill, one of the leaders of the cowboys, was shot and killed by Wyatt.

Lake, in his book, *Wyatt Earp, Frontier Marshal,* describes the encounter between Wyatt and Curley Bill Brocius at considerable length.[13] Earlier, Curley Bill and eight others had been deputized by Sheriff Behan to arrest Wyatt's group. By chance, Wyatt stumbled upon Curley's posse at Iron Springs, later known as Mescal Springs. The deputized outlaws opened fire on Wyatt and company but missed. Wyatt shot Curley Bill in the midsection with his shotgun. After an exchange of gunfire, both sides withdrew.

The outlaws for years denied that this gunfight occurred. They explained Curley Bill's disappearance by indicating that he had gone to Mexico to start a cattle ranch. Wyatt was quite certain that Curley could not have survived the shotgun blast. He knew that Curley was dead.

No one knew what happened to Curley Bill's body. It appeared that his companions buried him near where he fell. However, Ralph Looney, in his book, *Haunted Highways, The Ghost Towns of New Mexico*, tells the following tale.[14] The ghost town of Shakespeare, New Mexico, is located close to the Arizona border. In its heyday, Shakespeare was a mining town and stagecoach stop and the hangout of colorful characters such as the notorious gunslinger Curley Bill Brocius. He was described as a six-footer with a fondness for flaming red neckties. He loved to shoot coins from the quivering hand of anyone who would hold them.

Looney states that Curley Bill ran up against Wyatt Earp somewhere in Arizona and took a load of buckshot in the abdomen. He was brought back to Shakespeare and died in the general store. He may be buried in the basement of this store.

Curley Bill, the Clantons and the McLowrys were all noted gunmen and fast on the draw. The other outlaw leader, the legendary Johnny Ringo went into hiding. Ringo was considered by many to be one of the fastest draws on the frontier.

The posse then disbanded with Wyatt and Doc Holliday traveling to Colorado. Sheriff Behan tried to have Wyatt and Doc extradited to Tombstone to stand trial for the deaths of Frank Stilwell and Indian Charley. The Governor of Colorado refused extradition and the matter was closed.

Recently however, Glenn Boyer, in his new book *Vendetta*, reveals for the first time that Wyatt and Doc established alibis in Colorado as to their whereabouts and secretly traveled back to the Tombstone area to try to kill Ringo.15

There has always been a mystery concerning the death of Johnny Ringo. He was found sitting under a tree with a bullet hole in his head. The curious thing was that he was wearing his gunbelt upside down and his boots could not be found. In lieu of other information, the coroner scratched his head and ruled suicide. Now, historian and author Boyer relates that Wyatt and Doc tracked Ringo to his camp where Wyatt killed Ringo in a gunfight and placed his body near a trail where it would be found. They then returned to Colorado. However, some authorities have questioned this explanation.

The death of Johnny Ringo ended Wyatt's vendetta against his brother Morgan's killers and also ended the outlaws grip on Tombstone. The remaining outlaws fled the area in fear. Thanks to the Earp brothers and their friends, Tombstone became a relatively law abiding community. Josie Earp, in her book, *I Married Wyatt Earp*, alleges that Wyatt personally killed Frank Stilwell, Curley Bill Brocius and Johnny Ringo for killing his brother Morgan.[16]

To this day there are ill feelings toward the Earps in Tombstone. Many relatives of Wyatt's victims still reside in the area. In boothill cemetery, the tombstone over the cowboys killed at the OK Corral reads something like, "Murdered by the Earps."

There is no doubt that Wyatt, his brothers and Doc Holliday did undertake a vendetta against the killers of Morgan and the assailants of Virgil. While wearing badges they took the law into their own hands. But, what choice did they have? Their efforts to bring law and order to Tombstone were sabotaged by Sheriff Behan at every turn. Prisoners were even allowed to escape jail. Had they not hunted down the murderers, justice would not have been rendered. Did the ends justify the means? The vendetta did bring peace to Tombstone, Arizona.

A word should be mentioned concerning Clara S. Brown, who was probably the first woman reporter on the western frontier. Efforts to trace her background have been unsuccessful. She is thought to have been married and also sent dispatches in the form of letters to Los Angeles and San Francisco newspapers. In newspaper parlance, she may have been a "stringer" who contributed news items although not a staff member. She remains a mystery.

However, Brown was recognized by *San Diego Union* staff writer Joe Stone in a newspaper article, dated October 22, 1972, entitled, *When They Shot It Out At The OK Corral, The Union Was There*.17 The article follows:

"Ninety-one years ago, on October 26, 1881, there occurred in the town of Tombstone, Arizona Territory an event which has endured in Western history and legend at least as well as Custer's Last Stand.

The event has become known as the Battle or Gunfight of the OK Corral. If you were a subscriber to the *San Diego Union*, you were there. The newspaper had a correspondent in Tombstone at the time.

First news of the incident in Tombstone came to the readers of *The Union* the morning of October 28. On page one there was an unsigned five-inch story beneath the headline:

ARIZONA COWBOYS
Sanguinary Battle in the Streets of Tombstone;
The Gang Used Up.

The story told of 30 shots being fired in a battle in which were engaged on one side, City Marshal V.W. Earp, his brother Morgan and a J.H. Holliday, and on the other, Jim and Frank McLowery, "left gasping in the agonies of death and Bill Clanton, mortally wounded."

The Marshal, said the story, got a flesh wound in the calf of one leg and his brother Morgan was wounded in the shoulder.

Ike Clanton, one of the cowboys, was slightly wounded and was in jail.

Anyone who wishes can find variations and additions to that story, including the spelling of names, in infinite variety. According to John Clum, editor of the *Tombstone Epitaph* and mayor of

21

the city at the time, wrote a book of his experiences in 1929, the story was:

> "The adversaries were Marshal Wyatt Earp, his brother Virgil, Chief of Police, brother Morgan and Doc Holliday versus Ike and Billy Clanton, Frank and Tom McLowry and Billy Claybourne called the cowboys. The McLowry's and Billy Clanton were killed. Virgil and Morgan Earp were wounded."

Whatever the facts, readers of the *Union* were treated on the morning of November 3, 1881, to a story on the fight which, in modern newspaper language, is called a sidebar or backgrounder.

The story was in the form of a letter. It was signed Clara S. Brown. During 1880 and 1881, there were 17 letters from Tombstone in *The Union* signed by Clara S. Brown.

After December 13, 1881, there is a lapse of four years, then a final from Los Angeles dated December 29, 1885. Reading all of these letters, one gathers that Clara S. Brown was married and there with her husband. There is no hint of his occupation. She had been to San Diego and had, while here, written letters or stories for newspapers in the East.

Between the Tombstone letters and the single one from Los Angeles, it is plain that she was living in the East, possibly Boston.

John Gilchriese, retired former chief field historian of Arizona and now owner of a Western store in Tucson and the Wyatt Earp Museum in Tombstone, said the name of Clara S. Brown was well known in her time. She was particularly known in newspapers in the Midwest and East with which she corresponded, but he did not know she wrote for *The Union*.

He believes that she and her husband lived in a hotel during her stay in Tombstone. Other than that, she is a mystery." End of newspaper article.

The above photograph shows the Southern Pacific Railroad Station at Tucson, Arizona where Frank Stilwell was found shot to death on the morning of March 21, 1882. Stilwell was alleged to have been a suspect in the ambush death of Morgan Earp in Tombstone. It is now clear that Stilwell was killed by Wyatt and Doc Holliday. Collection of the authors.

Chapter Three
AFTER TOMBSTONE

Doc Holliday returned to Colorado where he eventually died in a Glenwood Springs tuberculosis sanitarium with his boots off. Wyatt and Josie then made the rounds of western mining camps. Wyatt earned his living buying and selling mining claims and gambling at card games like Faro. He apparently was not only an honest gambler, but a good one. Gambling at this time was a very respectable line of work. In those years almost all adult men gambled, including bankers and other pillars of the community.

Wyatt and Josie were in Texas for a short while. In her book, Josie relates how Wyatt bumped into the famous cattleman and gun-slinger, Ben Thompson in El Paso, Texas.18 Many consider Ben Thompson the most notorious gunman on the frontier. While Wyatt and Ben may have been adversaries in Wichita and Dodge City, they conversed as old friends.

There is little evidence as to the couples whereabouts after they left Tombstone in 1882 and their arrival in San Diego between 1885 and 1887. Most historians list their arrival date in San Diego as 1887. Richard Erwin in his book, *The Truth About Wyatt Earp* indicated that Wyatt came to San Diego in 1885.19 However, Erwin offers only a short, six sentence paragraph to describe his stay in San Diego. The San Diego City Directory of 1887 has the first official listing of Wyatt. He could very well have lived here a year or two prior to the 1887 listing.

Wyatt pretty much avoided Arizona as he felt there was still a warrant for his arrest over his vendetta. While in San Diego, he did slip over to the Arizona side of the Colorado River to inspect various mining districts. It wasn't until years later, when Wyatt was offered the position of Marshal of the Arizona Territory, that he learned the murder warrants had been withdrawn years before.

This also may have accounted for, in part, his keeping a low profile throughout his lifetime.

However, there are newspaper accounts of Wyatt, Josie and brother James arriving at the new gold camp at Coeur d'Alene, Idaho in 1884 just prior to their arrival in San Diego.[20] The *Spokane Chronicle* published an article by Eldon Coroch, dated June 20, 1959, with this heading, *Idaho Knew Wyatt Earp, Famed Lawman of the West Involved in Old Law Suits* . The article describes several lawsuits brought against Wyatt and friends for claim jumping at Coeur d 'Alene. Wyatt lost all of these lawsuits, except one. Wallace, Idaho records reveal that the Earp faction filed and located four lode mining claims named Consolidated Grizzly Bear, Dividend, Dead Scratch and Golden Gate. James Earp filed the Jessie Jay claim on May 29, 1884. The Earp group also purchased a large tent where they operated a saloon. Wyatt and James also operated the White Elephant Saloon in the nearby town of Eagle.

Advertisements in the July 11 and 18 issues of the Eagle City *Coeur d'Alene Weekly*, said, "The largest and finest saloon in the Coeur d'Alene, Earp Bros, proprietors, in the new Theston Building, Eagle City, Idaho. The finest brands of foreign and domestic liquors to be found in the United States." Other records in the area reveal that Wyatt, James and others, on April 7, 1884, paid Florence McCarthy $500.00 for ten acres of gold placer ground on Pritchard Creek, known as the Florence McCarthy claim. On the same day, Wyatt and James bought, for $2250.00, in Eagle City, one circular duck tent 50 feet in diameter and 45 feet high. The group apparently left Idaho by December, 1884.

Just prior to coming to San Diego, Wyatt spent time with his family at their home in Colton, near San Bernardino, California. His brother Morgan, killed at Tombstone, is buried here. Morgan was Wyatt's favorite brother. Earp relatives still reside in that area.

Hunters Hot Springs, Montana 1883: 1. ?, 2 - Wyatt Earp, 3 - Teddy Roosevelt, 4 - "Doc" Holiday, 5 - Virgil Earp, 6 - "Liver Eating Johnson, 7 - "Butch" Cassidy (Geo. Parker), 8 - "Sundance Kid" (Harry Longabaugh),

This may be the most important photograph to surface from the Western Frontier. It was found in an old Idaho Lodge prior to being demolished. Montana was a territory at this time and none of the lawmen had any jurisdiction. It apparently was used as a safe refuge and resting place. Hunter's Lodge is located in the Southeastern portion of Montana. John and Shari Rudy who discovered the photograph apparently took their find to the Idaho Historical Society, who made tentative identifications.

10 - "Bat" Masterson, 12 - Harry Britlan, 14 - Judge Roy Bean, 15 - Ben Greenough.

"Liver Eating Johnson" is the nickname of Jeremiah Johnson. After the Crow Indians murdered his wife and children, he vowed to kill as many Crow Indians as he could, and eat their livers. He was so successful that the Crow Chief sued for peace. It is a rather far stretch to think that this prominent group would assemble at the same place at the same time. But, truth is sometimes stranger then fiction. Donated it to the Gaslamp Historical Museum from the collection of John and Shari Rudy.

Chapter Four
WYATT IN BOOMING SAN DIEGO

Wyatt Earp and his wife Josie came to San Diego sometime between 1885 and 1887, and remained off and on until about 1896. There are conflicting stories as to the reasons why they came here. Stuart Lake states that Wyatt and Josie were in El Paso, Texas when they heard that San Diego was experiencing a land boom and was wide open.21 There is also some evidence that his brother Virgil had visited, or was living in San Diego, and influenced Wyatt to settle here.22 However, Josie has said that Wyatt came to San Diego with Bat Masterson, brother Virgil and his wife Allie. Lake also indicated in his book that Virgil and Allie resided in San Diego for several years.23 There is some evidence for this, as an undated newspaper clipping listed Virgil Earp as being elected a director of the Old Silver Gate Athletic Club in San Diego.24 Virgil and Allie apparently returned to the family home in Colton when the boom collapsed in 1888. In later years both Wyatt and Virgil visited San Diego in attempts to salvage some of their real estate holdings.

In any event, the Earps arrived in 1885-87. This date is verified by the 1887 *San Diego City Directory* which shows Wyatt listed as a capitalist and residing at the Schmidt Building at 946 3rd Avenue.25 Josie, in her book, indicated that the operator of this room and boarding house, Mrs. Eliza Burns, became a good friend and remained so for many years.26 This establishment was across the street from Horton Plaza. It is noteworthy that next door, on the corner of 3rd and D (now Broadway), was a Wells Fargo office. Many suspect that Wyatt, for years, served as an undercover agent for Wells Fargo. It is known that he rode shotgun on a number of Wells Fargo stages.

On May 8, 1995, the author interviewed Judy (last name unknown),who indicated that Wyatt, when he first arrived in San Diego stayed at the Bayview Hotel located at 12th and Island streets.27 This hotel, once a first class establishment, still stands today and is now called the Palms Hotel. Judy stated that her mother told her that when she was a child she saw Wyatt, and that he was a gambler.

Concerning San Diego in the late 1880s, Wyatt received reliable information as the city was on the verge of boom times. Prior to 1885, visitors to San Diego came by way of ship or stage. That all changed in the magic year of 1885 when the Santa Fe Railroad began service between Los Angeles and San Diego. From that point on, the population grew from 5000 in 1885 to 30,000 in 1887. In this same year over 1000 ships arrived, brimming with passengers. Boom time had commenced.

Taking advantage of the times, Wyatt invested heavily in real estate, mostly in prime areas. He owned the Hillcrest block bounded by 4th and 5th, University and Washington Streets. Old time San Diegan, Curry Archie Bachman, had this amusing story to tell about one of Wyatt's properties located at 2nd and Lewis Streets also in Hillcrest.28 This material was taken from Bachman's oral history, which was recorded by the San Diego Historical Society on March 8, 1961.

> "Wyatt Earp owned property just catty cornered across the street from our house. Earp's property was 150 by 150 feet and he had it enclosed all the way around with a five foot lath fence. My father and Wyatt got to be quite good friends and they would sit out there under the palm tree and talk.
>
> My father wanted to build a chicken house so he said that he would take every other lath off the fence and build the chicken coop. Then he wanted to build a fence around the leveled off area so the chickens could not get out and get over to the Earp property. So then he took the other laths

off and evened it up all the way around.

The next time Earp came down he and the old man sat out there and talked and Wyatt said, Joe, you must have had a windstorm here- half those laths are gone.. And Joe said, You never saw such a windstorm in your life! Wyatt said that he expected there would be a tornado or something next because he didn't expect to find any laths at all on the fence the next time he came down. And father said he didn't expect there would be a damn bit of fence left by then. And Wyatt said that it really didn't matter because he didn't want the property anyway." End of interview.

In the downtown area, Wyatt owned the lot at the northeast corner of Beech and Union Streets. According to State Senator and retired Superior Court Judge Hugo Fisher, Wyatt also owned the northern portion of the block where the US Grant Hotel now stands.29 As a young man, Fisher became a close friend of Wyatt's biographer Stuart Lake. Lake resided for many years in San Diego and was considered by many to be a San Diego writer, He and his wife resided in Mission Hills and at the US Grant Hotel for a long period.

Over the years Wyatt owned or leased at least four saloons and gambling halls in San Diego. The most famous was the Oyster Bar located in the Louis Bank Building (A beautiful four story Victorian structure, still standing at 837 5th Avenue). It has been reported that the owner was a distant relative of Wyatt's wife, Josie. This was one of the better known and frequented saloon/gambling halls in the city. One of the reasons for its popularity was that upstairs was a whorehouse called the Golden Poppy. The unique feature was that each room was painted a different color and each lady wore a dress the same color as her room. This building was restored by noted San Diego architect Don Reeves and remains one of San Diego's finest examples of Victorian architecture.

Another interesting feature of this hotel was its four floor tiered outdoor privy. Each floor had its own ramp to the "two-holer." During the refurbishing of this hotel, the owner, Don Reeves, dug up the old privy and recovered over three hundred items including a beautiful bronze doorhandle, all sizes of bottles, porcelain dolls, glass marbles, and clay and Meerschaum pipes.30

Another location was just south of the St. James Hotel on the corner of 6th and F Streets. It was reported that Wyatt ran the highest stakes faro game at this location. Another popular spot was a saloon at 951 4th Street, again across the street from Horton Plaza. The Plaza Pawn Shop now occupies this site in the original building. Wyatt could look out his boarding house window and observe his saloon directly across Horton Plaza. The last location was at the northwest corner of 6th and G Streets and little is known of its operation. There is a lack of information concerning Wyatt's San Diego business and other activities. Most of this information has been gleaned from official city and county records. Wyatt apparently did not own the buildings where he operated saloons and gambling halls. Most of these businesses were operated under lease arrangements.

While Wyatt kept a relatively low profile in San Diego, some of his activities were noted in the press. *San Diego Union* staff writer Craig MacDonald, in an article entitled simply, "Wyatt Earp," dated October 17, 1978 presented interesting impressions and anecdotes from older newspaper reports relating to Wyatt.31 Some of these are as follows: "Wyatt's heroic exploits in Kansas, Missouri and Arizona have been passed down from generation to generation. Yet there was another Wyatt Earp seldom remembered- an older, wiser gentleman who lived in San Diego and operated gambling halls; bought and sold urban property; refereed fights and owned racehorses." Another report that Wyatt was active as a referee of prize fights. " In 1890, Earp reportedly refereed a fight between

Billy Graham of San Francisco and Jack Sullivan of Oceanside at the old "D" Street Theatre.[32] When not officiating at fights or running his gambling dens, Earp earned a reputation with many as being kind to animals and children. The late Clarence Rand once recalled Earp eating at his mother's boarding home.[33]

> "One morning when he came in to have breakfast, I was attracted by the two guns he was wearing. I was eight at the time and began talking about guns. Wyatt asked, 'Would you like to play with one of these guns?' 'Yes' I said, 'Could I hold one of them?' He dumped the cartridges out of it and handed the gun to me. I thought that was something great to be holding one of those big six guns."

By 1896, Earp had gradually sold most of his San Diego investments-a decision he regretted years later when the same land went for greater sums.

That was not the last San Diego saw of Wyatt Earp, however. He continued to pop up frequently in this Southern California city.

In 1923, Earp visited the Silver Strand (near Coronado) where a popular tent city catered to vacationers. He was fond of playing cards along the Strand and whenever things got out of hand with an occasional rough-and-tumble gambler, Earp would personally see to it that order was restored with his still agile fists.

Veteran San Diego journalist Frank Macomber remembers bumping into the old peace officer when Macomber was but a lad of five, staying at the Strand.

The wide-eyed youngster inquired of the aged gunfighter, much to his parent's horror, "Did you really kill all those people?" Earp merely smiled, picked up the tot and bounced him on his knee.

Macomber said years later he ran into a former Earp acquaintance who presented a different viewpoint of the hero with children. The man said one night Earp's horse disappeared outside one of his gambling halls. A small boy located the horse and brought it back to the enraged former lawman who pistol whipped the lad, thinking it was he who stole the critter.

If this incident was true, it would probably do little to damage the heroic image of Earp painted by countless articles, television shows and movies. As Macomber said, "There's no use trying to change everybody's mind, now the movies have made a hero of him. Like a fellow once said, 'I've made up my mind, stop trying to clutter it up with facts'."

The area now known as the Gaslamp Quarter covers a major portion of the 1880s Stingaree District. Many old timers claim that the Stingaree area was as wild and dangerous as the Barbary Coast in San Francisco. The following colorful, descriptive material of the 1880s Stingaree District and downtown San Diego is taken from Adalaska Pearson's Oral History dated 1928.34 Pearson, in his later years known as the Mayor of Duckville, was in his youth a law enforcement officer for the area of National City to the Mexican border. He was in a unique position to observe the lawlessness of the region. His narrative paints a good picture of the conditions under which Wyatt operated and prospered. He knew Wyatt and provides information concerning his gambling activities that were, until this point, unknown. His narrative is unedited.

He begins: "An over abundance of money, speculations of every kind and the close proximity of the border brought thousands of the sporting element to the San Diego bay region and in 1887-88-89 there could be found in San Diego more questionable characters of both sexes, more professional gamblers, "con" and "sure-thing" men, "tin horn gamblers" and all round crooks than in any city of the like size in the world.

Naturally a city numbering 30,000 souls, drawn from the adventurous classes of the country, crazy with gambling fever developed from fortunes made in real estate, would gravitate toward every form of vice. Saloons and gambling houses existed everywhere. The notorious gun men, the Earp brothers, Virgil and Wyatt, of Tombstone, Arizona fame were probably most prominent among the gambling fraternity. Their establishment was on 6th street between E and F and "the sky was the limit" as the saying goes, in their faro game.

They (the Earps) also promoted and were "bosses" of all the entertainment at Tijuana on Sundays, where prize fights, bear and bull fights and every form of gambling took place on the Mexican side of the line under the trees near Messinger's Store and Saloon within a few feet of the boundary monument. Every known game of chance could be found every Sunday, running wide open on the streets, from the big wheel, rouge et noir and faro to the little elusive pea under the walnut shells. Gamblers, tourists, business men, toughs, and last but not least, the scarlet women could be seen there by the thousands. They congregated in such numbers on Sundays at Tijuana that trains on the National City and Otay Railroad were full. They came in such numbers that getting them back to Los Angeles was a problem. Many did not get back home until Tuesday or Wednesday.

Crime was rampant.

Murder, theft, robbery, fights and general licentiousness was the order of the day, hold-ups were a daily occurrence. Near the close of 1888, when the boom broke incendiarism or arson was so prevalent that the Pacific Assurance Union of 419 California Street, San Francisco with its various companies refused to assume any more risks in San Diego. There were 29 coroner's juries summoned in 18 months to hold inquests on persons found murdered, drowned or who suffered death under suspicious circumstances. The city jail in 1887-88-89 was in the basement under the Court House. This building is still standing at the corner of 5th and G Streets. Here city and county prisoners from drunks to murderers were herded together in one large room in the daytime. At night, those charged with felonies were placed in separate cells.

The writer, (Ad Pearson), was constable and deputy sheriff of National Township from 1886 to 1890 and had as my "bailiwick" or township all that territory from the city limits of National City on the north to Tijuana, thence east along the border line for about ten miles thence back to near the Cajon Valley taking in Tijuana, Otay, Sweetwater, Jamacha, then back to National City, consequently my Sundays during the summers of 1887-88 and 89 were pretty well taken up with looking after the rough element at Tijuana. The desecration of Sunday both at the line and in San Diego was certainly complete. Picnics at all the various resorts, Sweetwater Grove, Ocean Beach and La Jolla, open gambling, carousing, drinking, fighting, bull fighting, bears and half a dozen prize fights was the Sunday program at Tijuana all through the summer months with an aggregation of about as tough and lawless an element to handle as one could find. My experiences as an officer were interesting at times and frequently not a little exciting, but during all this period although there was congregated in the vicinity of San Diego many noted "gun men" and "killers" as the saying is there were very few gun plays of gun fights. The drawing of a weapon meant "using it" and while thousands of men carried weapons daily very few gun plays were made, for a gun play meant a killing.

But bloody fights and brawls on Sunday at the line were so common that no notice was taken of a fight in the open, although it might be within half a dozen feet of a gambling game which had hundreds of dollars risked on its cloth or device.

San Diego was in a class of its own in 1888 at the zenith of the great boom. With the border within fifteen miles of a city filled with thugs of every description and money as plentiful as it was, crime of every description was rampant and the police force at the time was small. Brave and efficient men comprised it in San Diego. Joseph Coyne for many years sheriff and deputy sheriff occupied the position of Chief of Police. He was an old miner, brought up on the frontier, a fine judge of a men and if an appointee under him didn't prove up he was promptly fired. Very few malefactors got away, as the detective squad was not only recruited from the ranks of the force of tried men, but comprised well known "dicks" from San Francisco who were drawn here by the love of adventure. San Diego was well handled especially the "Red Light" district— from Fourth and Market south to the bay. The block bounded by J and K and Fourth and Fifth Streets contained 21 saloons, out of a possible 75 in the city. The largest of these had about 40 beer tables, was owned and conducted by One-Eyed McInerney and was about as tough a "joint" as ever existed in any city. When patrolling the red light district officers traveled in twos and not very far apart. Saloons were open all night, the gambling houses the same. Dance halls and chop houses in the red light district never closed their doors, in fact business was better from midnight till 3:00 a.m. than earlier in the evening as the drunks were all "snowed under" by midnight and the uptown gamblers and sight seers never showed up to take in the town until the night was half spent. Those were great times, truly, and to one whose business as an officer compelled him to mingle with the rough and tough and criminal element, it proved not only exciting but interesting as well. The old days are gone and with them types of men this country will never see again congregated in this city.

The boom brought the talented and artistic, musicians, statesmen, writers, and globe trotters. Every class was represented, the eminent, divine, as well as the con man, the gun man from Texas and Arizona. Wyatt Earp and Big Bertha the confidence queen of the Pacific, jostled arms with the clergyman or statesman on Fifth Street, in crowds of people who thronged the streets daily by the thousands, hurrying by each other, trying to turn one dollar into two, each in his own "way." Business and professional men of national reputation conducting their business next door to or in the same building with a gambling hall or a gilded saloon with a round dozen white aproned bartenders.

Brass bands playing on every third corner, drawing crowds, while a real estate auctioneer sold town lots to the speculator, who cared not if the property he was bidding on consisted of a "water lot" half a mile out in the bay or was situated in John Doe's addition to San Diego, 30 miles out in the country. Silk hats and Prince Albert coats, rubbed elbows with the jumper or blouse of a longshoreman drawing his dollar and hour, each bidding on the same lot, God knows where, while the auctioneers cries, "Only $50 a lot am I bid these lots will bring you $100 next week, gentlemen!" And they did for weeks and the bubble expanded till "bang" it broke— vanished into thin air and the dollars with it.

"Excitement became a sort of lunacy and men persuaded themselves San Diego would soon cover an area which soberly measured was seen to be larger than that of London. Business property that had been selling a year of so prior to 1887 for $500 a lot, passed through the market at $1000 to $2500 a front foot. Rents swelled correspondingly. A small cottage, shabbily built, with cloth and paper partitions, readily rented for $60 per month. So general was the demand for homes and business quarters that the appearance of a load of lumber on a vacant lot drew a knot of people who wanted to lease the structure in advance. Then the lessee camped out nearby waiting a chance to move in. Land advanced daily in swelling price and fortunes were made on margins. A $5000 sale was quickly followed by a $10,000 transfer of the same property and in three months a price of $50,000 was reached.

Early in the spring of 1887 someone erected an immense tent on the corner of Third and

E streets, where the Knights of Pythias Hall now stands, and readily obtained $1.50 per night for lodgings which consisted of a cot bed, with pillow and a couple of blankets.

Hundreds of small tents covered dozens of vacant lots on the outskirts of the city and dozens of people walked the streets nightly or camped out in the open around a fire, unable to procure lodgings.

At one time in 1888 there were at least 40,000 people in San Diego City, according to the best information obtainable at that time. The Post Office with its meager supply of help was utterly unable to handle the paper mill and tons of it were taken to the bay front and dumped in the water. Early in 1887 Gus W. Jorres was appointed postmaster. He later resigned the office, giving as a reason, "Too much work, too little pay." End of interview.

Another interesting story concerning Wyatt's activities at the Mexican border is recorded in the following newspaper article that appeared in the *San Diego Union* on July 23, 1961. The writer was Jerry McMullen, Director of the Serra Museum.[35] His article is as follows:

Headline, *Wyatt Earp And The Great 100-Round Boxing Match*, followed by "When the word got around that there was to be a 100-round prizefight in San Diego, both press and pulpit all but went into orbit and the boys of the sporty set decided in some haste that perhaps it wasn't such a good idea after all- even if Wyatt Earp was to be the referee.

As early as spring of 1888 public opinion was a thing to be heeded rather than opposed. So the promoters decided to take their fight and Mr. Earp down to Tijuana, where people weren't so persnickety. The date was set for Sunday, May 6 and the National City and Otay Railroad got ready to put on special trains to the border. It was to be a big day for the town's sports. Not only would there be a bare knuckles prize fight there would be two of them and there would be cock-fights, a bullfight and a lassooing contest.

Then the comandante at Tijuana got nervous. The mob of fight-fans would greatly outnumber his tiny garrison and you can never tell what is going to happen when a lot of people go to some big event, get tanked up and start a rhubarb of their own. So he ruled that while the fight itself could be held in Tijuana, the spectators must remain on the American side of the line. On that day a rope was stretched more or less along the dividing line, to keep things in their proper place.

The bullfight was later described by the local press as mediocre. The cock-fight was described as worse, as was a half-hearted roping contest. Then the first pair of fighters, Gus Brown and Spider Kennedy, squared off. Spectators jeered when the bare-knuckles were found to be covered by skin-tight gloves. The two pugs, both imported from San Francisco, had at it, but it was no 100-round affair. Brown put Kennedy away in the sixth.

The next fight was between two locals, a blacksmith named William McLaughlin and a longshoreman James O'Neal. This one promised to be better. Not only did they fight with bare fists, but it was reported that there was bad blood between the pair and indeed they went after it with great energy. By the end of the fourth round the blacksmith was in bad shape and O'Neal had no trouble in landing one under the jaw which put him in dreamland for the next five minutes. So ended the great international event." End of article.

Wyatt Earp operated a saloon and gambling hall in this building in the 1880s. The Palace Pawnbroker now occupies the space. The building at 951 4th Avenue is across the street from Horton Plaza in the heart of downtown San Diego. From his saloon Wyatt could see his rooming house only one short block away on 3rd Avenue, across the Plaza. Collection of the authors.

This photograph shows the Horton Grand Hotel when it was located on F Street between 3rd and 4th. It was later demolished brick by brick and rebuilt on Island Avenue between 3rd and 4th. Courtesy Horton Grand Hotel.

This photograph shows the new and rebuilt Horton Grand Hotel located between 3rd and 4th on Island Avenue, Gaslamp Quarter, in downtown San Diego. It is now a first class and elegant hotel. Wyatt once occupied room 409. This was a favorite haunt. Collection of the authors.

This former bank building once housed the well known Oyster Bar and Gambling Hall that Wyatt operated on a lease basis from the owner, Isidor Louis (who may have been a relative of Josie Earp). This beautiful 1880s building, located at 837 5th Avenue, was renovated by owner and architect Don Reeves in recent years. The upstairs rooms were later known as the Golden Poppy and were occupied by shady ladies. This is an outstanding landmark in the Gaslamp District. Collection of the authors.

The Louis Bank Building as it looks today after restoration. Collection
of the authors.

This photograph shows the Tivoli Saloon where Wyatt spent much time during the 1880s. This bar is located on the northeast corner of 6th and Island Avenue. It is the oldest continuously operating bar in San Diego. Collection of the authors.

This photograph shows the interior of the Tivoli Bar and Grill as it looks today. This original wooden bar came to San Diego by sailing ship in the 1870s. The new owner is decorating the interior with Wyatt's photographs. Collection of the authors.

This is a famous photograph of San Diego in the 1880s. This is how the city looked when Wyatt strolled up 5th Avenue from Horton's pier on San Diego Bay. This was the center of business activity. By 1890, the respectable business district had moved eight blocks north, leaving only brothels, gambling halls and saloons. The area then became known as the Stingaree and was described as one of wildest Red Light districts in the West. Courtesy San Diego Historical Society, Photo Collection.

This excellent photograph shows the Schmitt Building on the left, where the Earps resided for a period of time. This may be the boarding house operated by Mrs. Eliza Burns with whom Josie became life-long friends. In the foreground is Horton Plaza located between 3rd and 4th on D Street (now Broadway). One of Wyatt's saloons was located approximately where the photograph was taken on 4th Ave. Courtesy San Diego Historical Society, Photo Collection.

G. B. GROW & CO., INSURANCE, REAL ESTATE

J. M. ROBINSON, ATTORNEY. Practices in all Federal and State Courts, Special attention given to defective titles of all kinds before the departments at Washington, D. C.

E

Eadon E. H., Post Office News Stand, P. O., res 1151 First
Eadon William H., Coroner, res 1151 First
Ealy Mrs. K., clerk, Commercial Hotel, res same
Earle Frank S., res 663 Eleventh
Earp Wyatt, capitalist, res Schmitt Block
East Public School, **S. D. LAND AND TOWN CO.'S** addn. Mary G. Phelps, teacher, third division; M. F. Hann, teacher, fourth division; Eliza Lundergreen, teacher, fifth division and principal.
Eaton A. C., contractor, res 1248 Fifth
Eaton Mrs. Fanny R., res 1803 B
Eaton Miss Flora, milliner, with Mrs. S. A. Williamson, res 1136 Fourth
Eaton G. F., elevator man Consolidated Natl Bank Building, res 1803 Ninth
Eaton Miss G. F., clerk with Consolidated Natl Bank, res cor Ninth and B
Eaton Miss Katie, cigar store, 755 Fifth, res Roxbury
Eaton W. C., lodging house, 530 Sixth, res same
EASTON, ELDRIDGE & CO., real estate, F. B. Wilde, local manager, San Francisco
Eausulchkat D., carpenter, res F ave bet 7th and 8th, Coronado
Ebirhart Obie C., scavenger, order box, N. W. cor. Fifth and J, res 1322 India
EBRIGHT F. R., collection agency, rooms 31 and 34, Bakesto Block, res same
Eckenrode J. C. H., carpenter, res 606 Julian

Rememcer that MARSTON keeps
NOVELTIES IN DRESS GOODS AND SILKS

MAISON RICHE, Finely Appointed PRIVATE DINING ROOMS Geo. Vigneron, Prop. Fourth, opp. Plaza

This page from the San Diego Register of 1887 or 1889 shows Wyatt Earp listed as a capitalist and residing at the Schmitt Boarding House. This residence was located near 3rd and Broadway, across the street from Horton Plaza. Collection of the authors.

Chapter Five
WYATT IN SAN DIEGO, COLLAPSE OF BOOM

For a vivid and unedited description of the business collapse we again return to the reminiscences of Adalaska Pearson.

He states, "About the middle of the year 1888, hard times commenced to be felt in the city. Real estate had reached its apex in value. To those who participated in the general excitement during boom days and who are still with us, the memory of the collapse of the boom is painful.   It can be said that people seemed possessed with a mild sort of insanity during the boom. Any scheme which promised return found hundreds of investors.

The first symptom of the fall in values in real estate holdings commenced when those who were speculating in margins offered theirs at a discount, small, but enough to throw a scare into the market.

Then the value of city and county real estate dropped and kept dropping. It was impossible to borrow money from the banks of the city as it is estimated that nearly $2,000,000 was withdrawn from deposits within a year's time. Those who were able to close their holdings at a small loss did so and faded away. By the middle of 1889 the city had lost nearly 10,000 in population. The establishment of a new bank in 1889, the San Diego Trust and Savings Bank, failed to restore confidence. Building of every description stopped—dozens of buildings, some very pretentious were never completed. All public improvements came to a standstill.

In the courts thousands of foreclosure proceedings were filed and hard times among all classes was here. Thousands of mechanics with families were unable to get employment. Many of these had purchased lots and erected little houses for homes, paying for them monthly. With no work and no credit it is easy to see the result. There was actually suffering among those who had lost their little all and were unable to raise money enough to get away. And in all Southern California it was the same. Values in Los Angeles and San Bernardino counties dropped as rapidly as in San Diego. City property which could have been readily sold in 1887 for $50,000, or $100,000 could not be mortgaged in 1889 for $10,000. Everyone seemed to be broke. Outsiders who had speculated largely in 1887 and who realized when the apex of good times and ready money had been reached, sold out and silently stole away.

Thousands of investors were left land poor, holding real estate contracts with one or two installments paid up and absolutely unable to meet the remainder. Failure after failure occurred among the large business houses, consequently hundreds of small stores went to the wall.

Fire after fire occurred not only business houses but dwellings until in early 1888 the Fire Assurance Union of San Francisco with Chas. D. Haven as secretary, instructed the leading insurance companies to assume no risks in San Diego and offered a reward of $500 for the arrest and conviction of anyone committing arson in San Diego. At that time the writer was Constable of National City and Township, which extended to the Mexican line.

Times were just as stringent there as in San Diego and fires just as frequent. I was fortunate in detecting a couple of fire bugs in the act and although the Assurance Union's reward read "for detecting arson in San Diego City" the company promptly mailed me a check through Beermaker and Shawbut of National City for half the reward of $250. This was in October of 1888 and my work as an officer in this case helped greatly to re-elect me to the same office on the presidential ticket of Ben Harrison that year.

Times went from bad to worse. In 1890 it was estimated the population of the city had dwindled to 20,000 people. Hundreds of old timers had left the city. Men who two short years previous could have their checks for $100,000 honored by the banks were flat broke. There was no credit. Hard times had indeed come to San Diego.

There was much suffering among the poor. Shipping business had quit cold. The longshoreman's union, one of the strongest on the coast, disbanded and its members scattered, like hundreds of other residents of the city.

Dwellings and business houses were burglarized nightly. Hold ups of almost daily occurrence. In the latter part of 1889 there were nearly 100 prisoners in the county jail awaiting trial, nearly all for felonies. The criminal calendar had 1800 cases on record and although there were three superior court judges in office from 1888 to 1890 (Judges Aiken, Puterbaugh, and Pierce) the civil and criminal calendars were so filled with cases awaiting trial that unless a party charged with a felony or was able to give bail he was compelled to remain in jail for about six months awaiting trial. There were hundreds of fine dwellings empty. Hundreds of residents also owned fine homes were compelled to leave the city, taking their families and going elsewhere to engage in business or obtain employment.

As there was no demand for houses they were simply forced to leave them vacant. In 1890 a certain prominent attorney who was forced to leave the city on account of lack of business, in my presence offered a friend the use of his fine house, furnished, for a year if he would live in it, look out for repairs and pay the water bill to keep up the law. And, the offer was declined with this words, "I've got to get away myself and am willing and anxious to make the same deal concerning my home with any responsible party."

The failure of the California National Bank about the latter part of 1891 followed by the suicide of its cashier and the flight of its vice president, was a financial shock to many San Diegans. The bank finances were in such a shape that the failure was complete. The depositors received little or nothing when the bank affairs were settled by the receiver.

Business in the city was at a standstill, and when in 1893 the Consolidated National Bank, one of San Diego's oldest banks, closed its doors and went into the hands of a receiver, confidence in the city's future prosperity seemed lost indeed. In 1890 I doubt if there were 16,000 bona fide residents in San Diego. About this time there was such a dearth of employment in the city that to relieve actual suffering the city council passed an ordinance authorizing the superintendent of streets to employ bona fide residents with families to clean the streets of all debris. This gave employment to some hundreds of old residents and although the pay was very small it relieved many from actual want and suffering. How the businessmen of the latter eighties who had faith in San Diego's ultimate success and prosperity have been repaid is learned by referring to the magnificent building just completed on the corner of 6th and Broadway by the San Diego Savings Bank, with MT Gilmore one of the founders as president; the department store of The Marston Company, Hardy's Packing House and Market; the grocery store of M.E. Heller on 5th street near E, with its 30 odd branches, the Hamilton Grocery Co. corner 6th and C, or Klauber, Wagenheim Co., all pioneer firms of over 40 years standing.

From the year 1890 to the opening of a new century in 1900 San Diego's future as one of the leading cities of southern California looked dreary indeed. The national census of 1890 showed nearly 17,000 population. That of 1900 gave San Diego a little over that figure. During these ten years business was at a standstill, not only here but throughout the entire country." End of interview.

While Wyatt was stuck with several properties, he prospered with his saloons and gambling halls. Gambling sometimes grossed a thousand dollars a day. During the heyday of the boom, he won a trotting horse, called Otto Rex, from a Mr. Jim Leach during a poker game at E.B. Gifford's place. This was the start of an almost ten year period of where Wyatt and Josie travelled the western racehorse circuit. They even traveled to Chicago and St. Louis with their small stable. Josie has indicated that both she and Wyatt fell in love with racehorses and racing. Wyatt formed a racing partnership with Gifford who was an old Tombstone friend. Gifford later served in the Arizona legislature for a number of years. He and two others donated the land on which the University of Arizona now stands.

Wyatt started racing here in San Diego at the old Turf Club in Pacific Beach. He also raced locally at Tijuana and Escondido tracks. Later they raced at San Francisco, Santa Rosa, Napa, Exposition Park in Los Angeles and Santa Ana. On several occasions, Wyatt drove his own rubber-tired sulky and on one occasion won a race.

During this period, Wyatt met the famous and immensely wealthy Lucky Baldwin and his daughter Clara Baldwin Stocker. Lucky was one of the Comstock Mining Lode millionaires and well known on the West coast. His name was constantly in the newspapers due to his flamboyant behavior and his womanizing. Two of his victims actually shot him. One, a cousin, shot him after claiming that he had "ruined her body and mind." In another incident he was accused of seducing a young girl, and while in court, was shot by the victim's sister. Lucky kept the scandal sheets in business. He and Wyatt were friends and shared a love of horse racing.

The Belle View Rooming House, one of Josie and Wyatt's first San Diego homes, was located at the northeast corner of 4th and G Streets. The original building, located in the Gaslamp District, is long gone. Collection of the authors.

This restaurant, located at the NW corner of 6th and F Streets, is where Wyatt is alleged to have operated a gambling hall. He may have also operated another gambling hall just north of this location and next store to the St. James Hotel. Collection of the authors.

This is the Palm Hotel located at the NE corner of 12th and Island Avenue where Wyatt lived for a short time. In the 1880s, this hotel was known as the Bayview Hotel and was considered first class. Collection of the authors.

Chapter Six
AFTER SAN DIEGO

It is difficult to pin down the date when Wyatt left San Diego because he retained property here well into the mid 1890s. It was reported in the *San Diego Union* on February 1, 1894 that Wyatt was sued for recovery of a promissory note payment.36 Still later, on April 15, 1908, a small item appeared in the *San Diego Union* as follows: *City Made Defendant In Middletown Lot Suit*, Plaintiffs Say Land Sold for Taxes Belongs to Them".37 It continues, "Wyatt Earp filed a complaint in the superior court yesterday in which the city of San Diego is named as one of the defendants." The rest of this newspaper article lists the other defendants and pertains to lot 8, block 17, in Middletown.

Wyatt traveled extensively with his racing activities and refereed boxing matches up and down the coast. As noted earlier, Wyatt and Josie formed a close relationship with Lucky Baldwin and his daughter. Baldwin built the famous Baldwin hotel in San Francisco, developed Lake Tahoe and purchased the Santa Anita Ranch where he built the famous race track of the same name. Wyatt and Josie lived in the lap of luxury while in Lucky's company. Josie stated that she and Wyatt were married on Lucky's yacht although no records were ever found.38 On a racing trip to Chicago with Lucky Baldwin, Wyatt introduced Josie to Buffalo Bill, whom he had met during his Buffalo hunting days in Kansas.

Josie also indicated in her memoirs that she and Wyatt settled in the old Bay District of San Francisco where their horse stables were located.39 Josie's parents lived there and she had relatives in Oakland. They apparently raced rather extensively at bay area tracks, as they established their own racing colors, navy blue polka dots on a white field. She reported that the well known jockey, Ted Sloan, once rode two of their horses to victory on the same day.

57

Several years ago an old timer came into my bookshop and claimed that his father, a jockey, had ridden several races for Wyatt Earp at Bay Meadows or Tanforan in the 1890s.40 He related that his dad was standing next to two well dressed men when one stated, "I wish I could find a jockey that could stay on a horse." His dad spoke up and said "I'm your man." Wyatt Earp hired him on the spot. The old timer didn't say how things worked out.

It was while in the Bay area, in 1896, that Wyatt refereed the infamous heavyweight bout between Tom Sharkey and Bob Fitzsimmons. The newspaper accounts indicate that Fitzsimmons knocked Sharkey out of the ring, but Wyatt awarded the fight to Sharkey on a foul, claiming that Fitzsimmons threw a low blow. The backers of Fitzsimmons were outraged and cried "bribe." This is the same fight where Wyatt wore a big colt revolver into the ring. Later that evening he was arrested for carrying a concealed weapon, released on bond and later fined. The US Boxing Commission, on the basis of this incident, passed a rule prohibiting referees from being armed while in the ring which is still in force today.

In a press release, dated April 5, 1896 at San Francisco, the follow-up story is reported.41

> "Tom Sharkey is still confined in his bed. His physicians say he will be up in a few days, no worse for the blow that secured him $10,000. Fitzsimmons is cheerful and he says he will get the purse yet. However, Lynch, Sharkey's backer ridicules Fitzsimmons expectations.

> Bets on the fight are being paid off today. Some pool sellers settled yesterday. One bookmaker paid out $28,000 this afternoon to holders of Sharkey's tickets." End of news article.

Another press dispatch on the same day, entitled "Philosophical Reflections, Wyatt Earp the most talked of man of the hour," takes a philosophical view of the criticisms that are being heaped upon him for his decision and he says he will wait for time to set him right with the public.42 "If I had any fears that I erred in my decision they would disappear today when I saw Sharkey." Apparently some accused Sharkey of also committing a low blow which Wyatt is quoted as saying,

> "Sharkey did not strike a foul blow, to my mind. At the break he struck Fitzsimmons as soon as his arm was free. But that is following Queensbury rules. It was agreed that there would be no fighting at the break. My instructions from the club were not to be technical, but to give the audience a good fight for the money.
>
> I have no regret about the whole matter, that is, that I did not leave the ring when Julian objected to me. I thought of doing it but it occurred to me that it would be showing yellow to do that. I would be quitting under fire and I made up my mind to stay until ordered off by the club. I am sorry that I acted as referee at all.
>
> The only inconvenience Fitzsimmons is suffering as a result of his meeting with the sailor is a painful swelling of the joints of the hands. I have nothing more to say in explanation," he said. End of article.

It is interesting that Wyatt received a word of support from former law enforcement friends in Wichita, Kansas, as the following press report shows:

> "Wyatt Earp the referee of the Fitzsimmons/Sharkey fight was a policeman in

Wichita under the notorious chief of police Mike Meagher.43 Dick Cogell who succeeded Meagher as chief says Earp is a man who never smiled or laughed. He was the most fearless man I ever saw. He was Marshal at Ellsworth, Kansas when that was a cattle shipping point and he was a success. He is an honest man. All officers here who were associated with him declare that he is honest and would have decided according to his belief in the face of an arsenal." End of news article.

This is a rather remarkable vote of confidence and support. There are many Earp haters, both in his day and now. I have had old timers visit my museum collection of Earp memorabilia and come out swearing and putting down all of the Earps as whoremongers, crooked gamblers and thieves. When questioned as to where or how they formed these strong opinions, they could not answer. Part of the answer may result from the fact that most Earp supporters in Tombstone left soon after the Earps departed, which coincided with the mines playing out and a general decline in business. The folks who remained were mostly cattlemen, rustlers, and the kin of the men killed by the Earps at the OK Corral. There are still hard feelings in Tombstone today.

Chapter Seven

ALASKA GOLD RUSH - YUKON, NOME

Wyatt and Josie were on a trip to Yuma, Arizona when the news broke that gold had been discovered in Alaska. Two ships from Alaska arrived in Seattle and San Francisco, each carrying hundreds of rich miners loaded with gold dust and nuggets. There was at least a ton of gold on each ship.

The country in 1897 was experiencing a severe depression. Many people were near starvation, due to high unemployment. There was no welfare in 1897. You either worked or went hungry. The news that any man could pick up gold nuggets in streams fired the imagination of everyone. Robert Service, in his autobiography, *Ploughman Of The Moon*, stated that the lure of gold affected men all over the world.44 Gold was the magnet that drew thousands to the Klondike, from nobleman to laborer. It has been described as the greatest gold rush of all time. For many it became a frenzy.

Robert Service, shortly after the gold rush, became overnight the favorite poet of millions of men. Service stated in his autobiography that he sent his first poems to a publisher from White Horse in the fall of 1906. The poems, very reminiscent of Rudyard Kipling, described with great beauty the magnificence of the arctic and the humor of the miners. The book was called *The Spell Of The Yukon*.45 The rhyme and cadence were ideal for reciting out loud. Particular favorites were *The Shooting Of Dangerous Dan McGrew* and *The Cremation Of Sam McGee.*

During the winter of 1906-07, the publisher issued many editions which spread throughout the world. It is claimed that by 1907 every single English speaking bar in the world had as evening entertainment someone reciting Service's poems. The practice of men memorizing these poems continued until after World War II. The author remembers men who had memorized dozens of Service's poems, reciting them with great gusto in army barracks, in Red Cross canteens and in combat areas in the Pacific during World War II.

Back to the story. Wyatt and Josie immediately returned to San Francisco. Here, they outfitted for the trip to Juneau, Alaska. Enroute, Josie learned she was pregnant. She had miscarried once before and was fearful of suffering another misadventure. They immediately booked passage back to San Francisco. Unfortunately, she also lost this child. This was their last chance at parenthood.

Within a few months they returned to the gold rush and hoped to make Dawson City by riverboat. But it was late in the season and they only made it to Rampart City before being snowed in for the winter. Luckily, they found a cabin which they rented from noted author Rex Beach. Josie indicates in her reminiscences that she and Wyatt enjoyed the arctic winter. They made friends in the small community which included Tex Rickard, the future famous fight promoter. In later years, Tex made Jack Dempsey famous and built Madison Square Garden in New York City. They also met and socialized with some of the well-known pioneers of the area.

With the spring thaw, they learned that business and prospecting possibilities in Dawson City were not promising. They then decided to try Nome where another recent gold discovery had been made. Enroute to Nome they stopped at Saint Michael, where Wyatt invested in a canteen that sold only beer and cigars. His profit here averaged $200.00 per day. They were content with this profit, but Tex Rickard persuaded them to come to Nome where the pickings were better.

In 1899 they did move to Nome where gold was actually found in beach sand. Wyatt immediately bought a lot in town and constructed a saloon called the Dexter. With the approach of winter and no decent housing they returned to San Francisco. Wyatt purchased furniture for his saloon and in the spring returned to Nome.

His Dexter saloon was soon one of the best and the most popular. He apparently opened a second saloon in Nome and shrewdly advertised it as the only "second class saloon in Alaska". Business boomed. Nome proved to be old home week for Wyatt. He met many of his old friends including John Clum and Lucky Baldwin. Clum, you will recall, was the first mayor of Tombstone and editor of the *Tombstone Epitaph* newspaper. He was truly a courageous man and Wyatt's lifelong friend. In Alaska, Clum organized the first U.S Postal system.

Lucky Baldwin's luck was running out. He had originally struck it rich in the great mining bonanza on the Comstock Lode. He came to the mining districts of Alaska to try and restore his tottering fortune. The following story pertaining to Wyatt is related in C.B. Glasscock's biography, *Lucky Baldwin*.46 When Lucky reached Nome, he was told that a bunch of crooked officials infested the local gold fields and had a scheme to control all businesses and property. This crooked scheme was well documented in Rex Beach's best selling novel, *The Spoilers*.47 The United States marshal confirmed that he would have to put up a ten thousand dollar bond on any property that he purchased as there was a lien on all property based on phony tax evasion charges. Lucky didn't have the ten thousand. He then went to Wyatt with his problem.

Wyatt assembled several friends and arranged the bond. When Lucky took the bond to the United States marshal he was told it was no good and that he would have to present twenty thousand in gold dust. Lucky went back to Wyatt, who, madder then hell, got together the gold and even had a friend lug it over to the marshal's office where the property was released.

Lucky later sold this property for a profit of fifty thousand dollars. He stated that Wyatt refused a cent of pay for his efforts. Wyatt is reported to have said, " I was more than satisfied to put a crimp in the grafting of that crowd of crooks". It is interesting to note that Lucky Baldwin described downtown Nome's liquor and

There is a degree of mystery concerning this photograph. It was taken by noted photographer E.A. Hegg and appears in *One Man's Gold Rush, A Klondike Album,* by Murray Morgan, Univ. Washington Press, 1967. Hegg labeled this photograph, "Wyatt Earp owned 'the Only Second Class Saloon in Alaska' at Nome." In his biography, Lucky Baldwin describes this saloon by this name and indicated it belonged to Wyatt. Most historians describe Wyatt's saloon in Nome as the Dexter. Perhaps he owned two saloons. Courtesy Special Collections Division, University of Washington Libraries, Hegg, 3019.

gambling as centered around Wyatt's Second Class Saloon. A few blocks from Earp's saloon, in any direction, business simply petered out. Wyatt and Lucky were friends to the end.

During the 1960s, the author became acquainted with and interviewed Doc Kearns, the manager of heavyweight champion Jack Dempesy.48 Doc was staying at light heavyweight champion Archie Moore's home in San Diego. He spent many evenings at Bob Johnston's Sports Bar, which was located on F Street between 3rd and 4th, next to the Hollywood Burlesque Theater. These Gaslamp buildings were razed to make way for the new and innovative Horton Plaza shopping mall. This included the Horton Grand Hotel where Wyatt spent many nights. This beautiful hotel was moved, brick by brick, to its present location on Island, between 3rd and 4th Streets in downtown San Diego. Present owners, Mr. and Mrs. John Rose, prominent citizens, have also recreated Bob Johnston's Sports Bar in the hotel. The hotel occasionally gives tours of Wyatt's old room #409.

Doc liked to reminisce and related many stories of his and Jack's travels and adventures. He recalled that he and Jack met Wyatt in his saloon in Nome. He confirmed the many well-known personalities that hung out in Wyatt's place. This was the best saloon in Nome. Some of these persons included writers Jack London and Rex Beach and mining engineer, Herbert Hoover. Hoover, prior to being elected President, was the premier mining engineer in the world. How about that for name dropping?

Another prominent character that Wyatt met at Nome was Walter Scott, known as Death Valley Scotty. Scotty in later years claimed to have found a gold mine located somewhere in the Death Valley region. He was a big spender and frequently was seen throwing money around in saloons up and down the West Coast. He financed a record setting railroad run from Los Angeles to Chicago by the Santa Fe. The railroad track, from Los Angeles to Chicago, was cleared of all freight and passenger trains allowing the Scotty

Express to set this record which, to this day, has never been surpassed. The feat has gained legendary status. According to a Santa Fe publication the time was 44 hours and 54 minutes.49 It was front page news across the nation. Scotty became famous and later built a palatial mansion in Death Valley that is now referred to as " Death Valley Scotty's Castle." It is now common knowledge that a wealthy Chicago businessman financed Scotty's many exploits, not a secret gold mine.

The following newspaper article describes an unusual interview with Wyatt, where he calls Scotty a faker. This was reported in the *San Diego Union* of March 25, 1906.50 The headline reads, *Calls Scotty A Rank Faker, Wyatt Earp Says That Death Valley Man Has No Mine—Met Him Once In Alaska As Breckenridge.* The rest of the article follows:

> "Wyatt Earp, one of the famous Earp brothers of Arizona and for many years a resident of Colton and San Bernardino and one of the best officers that ever pulled a gun on a bad man, is living in Los Angeles and has given the following to the *Record* on his meeting with Scotty in Alaska.
>
> Late one evening I was seated in my saloon talking with a friend when five rough looking characters jostled in and ordered drinks. They were as tough appearing a bunch as a man would meet in a long time, but I thought nothing of that as we served hundreds of bad men and never had any trouble. After putting away several drinks apiece the men went over to one corner of the canteen and began to talk in a whisper.
>
> I did not pay much attention to them, but finally heard one of them say in an excited tone. You better not throw my home was only a minute's walk

worst of it. [This last sentence must be a misprint by the newspaper as it does not make sense. Ed.]

I didn't have my gun with me but my home was only a minute's walk from the saloon and I sent one of my assistants to the house to tell Mrs. Earp that I had taken in $600 or $700 that day and to send my gun down.

Scotty who was one of the gang, then sauntered over to me and looking me square in the face, said I don't give a —— for bull, but I admire you just the same. That was all right and we shook hands.

The party stayed around a little while longer and then left, leaving a negro behind. They had been gone but a few minutes when the negro came over and said 'Do you know who that feller was that was speaking with you? And I told him no. Well, that feller is the guy that murdered that Frenchman at St. Michaels, six months ago and got away with $16,000. He a member of the Black Jack gang of New Mexico and left there when things got too warm. The Black Jack gang separated and Breckenridge thought it pretty safe up here.

I immediately recalled the murder of the Frenchman one night, the arrest of the murderer and his escape from prison.

The stranger left Rampart that evening and I thought no more of the incident until I met Walter Scott in the Hollenback bar about one year ago and at once recalled the incident in my canteen in Alaska. Unless my judgement of human nature is poor, Walter Scott of Death Valley fame and Breckenridge are one and the same person.

I do not like to say anything against a fellow when he's down as I have been in trouble myself and know what it means. I do not think that Scotty has a mine in Death Valley, as I have prospected all through it for the past twenty years and knew that no man could have a mine there and others not know it. He has no more of a mine than I have and not as much for I have a mine just on the outskirts of the valley.

I think he is a great faker and when he failed to dispose of stock for his mine in New York he decided that a theatrical career was the next best."
End of interview.

The Earps left Nome in 1901 prosperous. It is estimated that they returned to the states with at least $80,000. They were wealthy for awhile.

This proves that there is a Earp, California named by the US Postal Service in honor of Wyatt. The Earp sign belongs to the Santa Fe Railroad. The track continues to Parker, Arizona on the Colorado River, a mile distant. Posing is old friend Mike Sullivan who visited Wyatt's mining claims nearby. Collection of the authors.

Chapter Eight

WYATT AS PROSPECTOR AND MINER

After Nome, Wyatt and Josie followed the gold rushes to Tonopah and Goldfield, Nevada. These two major gold strikes were the last in US Territory. They left from Los Angeles with a horse drawn wagon filled with camping equipment . They climbed Cajon pass, proceeded to Barstow, Needles and Las Vegas, then north to Tonopah, Nevada, camping out all the way.

At Tonopah in 1902, Wyatt financed the Northern Saloon and again made considerable money. He rubbed shoulders with many of his cronies from Alaska and Tombstone. His brother Virgil also came to Tonopah. In 1905, Virgil Earp died of pneumonia at Goldfield, eight miles south of Tonopah, ending a distinguished law enforcement career. He was a good man.

During this interval Wyatt and Josie began to prospect in earnest. They would leave Tonopah for weeks at a time on prospecting trips. They were on the right track because around 1908 a major gold strike was made just eight miles south of Tonopah. This new discovery called Goldfield rivaled Tonopah's mines in richness. It appears Wyatt was a miner and prospector at heart.

Wyatt eventually sold out his interest in the Northern Saloon and returned to Los Angeles. Again, he made a handsome profit.

The spring of 1903 found them again prospecting in the desert. Josie reported that she once found a piece of gold float (rock) that appeared very rich. They searched in vain for the vein in which it originated. However, this spurred them on to look for other "finds."

It is interesting that a *Los Angeles Record* newspaper article was reprinted by the *San Diego Union*, date unknown, and reported the following heading, *Wyatt Earp starts out for Goldfields, Nevada, Former San Diegan walked all over that camp and passed it up.*51 This is the heading of the article. One can speculate that Josie found her rich piece of gold ore in the Goldfield area where a major gold discovery was made. Over $100,000,000. in gold was mined here. Wyatt and Josie could have walked over these riches without knowing it.

The rest of this newspaper article is presented as it shows how Wyatt was viewed by the mainstream press in the early 1900s. "He has some claims nearby which he now thinks will pan out well. Wyatt Earp is afield once more," comes the news from the *Los Angeles Record.*

"The man of a hundred gun fights departed for Goldfield, Nevada with a full wagonload of camp supplies and will take a month or six weeks for the trip.

The only visible relic of the old Wyatt Earp is his Winchester 73 which he carried up from the Pacific Coast with him. From Nome to Calico for fifteen years his trusty gun is only taken along on the chance that he may come upon some game on the trip.

Wyatt is a gunfighter no more and has forsaken the green cloth and the faro bank for the life of a miner.

He intends to develop and prospect a few claims which he owns in the Old Frog District near Goldfield. The old Earp flashes out once in a while and the years spent in the public now serves him in good stead now that he is making another overland trip.

He says that he "will never shoot at another man again unless he shoots at me first. All I want is to make a stake on some of my claims and that what I am making the trip for.

I've located several good prospects when I was in Goldfields three years ago. But I walked right over the Goldfield ground and didn't even know there was anything in it." Wyatt Earp is past sixty years of age. For years he and his brothers ran Arizona to themselves. Finally one brother was killed and the rest returned to the paths of their own choosing. Whenever there was a new gold field or a new oil field in a new place in which money was plentiful there could be a Wyatt Earp. Quiet, careful but certainly in his own defense, Dawson, a cocky Canadian police officer attempted to presume on his own the moment Earp arrived that he told Earp that no gun play would be tolerated. For those who heard the quiet old voice of Wyatt Earp on that occasion say they never heard any living man get a dressing down in quite such language as did that police officer. Earp can be quiet and he has been very like Bat Masterson and others of the old six shooter school. He prefers peace and quiet and men of that class usually get what they want." End of news article.

It is interesting that this reporter mentioned Wyatt's Winchester rifle, as Stuart Lake, several years later, wrote a screen play entitled *Winchester 73*, which starred Jimmy Stewart but had as minor supporting roles actors playing Wyatt, Virgil and Bat Masterson. The film was considered the best western of the year.

In later years, Wyatt and Josie prospected the California desert at Vidal near the Colorado River. In early years this was easy traveling to and from Los Angeles. They would take the train to Yuma, Arizona and than travel by steamboat up the river and prospect the southern fringes of the Whipple Mountains. Later they traveled by the Santa Fe Railroad to Needles and then proceeded south by wagon. They would return to Los Angeles during the summer to avoid the oppressive desert temperatures. In the winter they would return to the desert.

In 1906 near the town of Vidal, Wyatt found several veins that contained both gold and copper. He had samples assayed and the ore appeared profitable for mining. They filed mining claims and called them "Happy Days." Over the years they filed dozens of claims with different names. The record of their mining can be viewed at the San Bernardino Hall of Records. Unfortunately, the good ore was on the surface and did not persist to any depth.

By sheer coincidence, my brothers Herb and Don Cilch visited the Earp claims in the late 1940s, just a little over twenty years after Wyatt last worked this mining property. My father, Colonel J.H. Cilch, along with my brothers, had made a similar copper/ gold discovery about twenty miles south of Needles, California. The discovery was an exceptionally large quartz vein that we traced off and on for one half mile. We called this claim the Cilch Santa Fe and it is still plotted on some maps of the area.

We were sure that this vein continued for a long distance or that a contact system continued where copper and gold would periodically outcrop on the surface. Several miles south of our location was located an older mine called Blue Boy which contained good copper ore. On a map we plotted the line of our outcrop with the Blue Boy which ran southeast and then proceeded to prospect along this line which led us to Wyatt's Happy Days claims. We did not linger as the ore at Wyatt's claim appeared to be low grade and not profitable.

In 1996 my brother Herb, an old buddy Mike Sullivan and one

This photograph shows Wyatt and Josie's cottage in Vidal, California. This may be the only house that the couple ever owned and lived in.. It was located close to their mining claims in the foothills of the Whipple Mountains. Vidal is now virtually a ghost town. Collection of the authors.

This photograph was taken from Wyatt's mining claim and shows the surrounding desert area with the Whipple Mountains in the background. Collection of the authors.

This is the opening of a mine shaft located on Wyatt's claim in the desert near Earp, California. Wyatt was following a vein of copper and gold ore. Collection of the authors.

of the authors revisited the Happy Days group of claims that are located on Highway 62, about half way between Vidal Junction and Parker Dam on the Colorado River. The claims are fairly easy to locate as they lie less than a mile north of the Vidal Junction/Parker Road. As you drive east from Vidal Junction, look for a brownish, volcanic lava intrusion that rises a hundred feet or more from the surrounding desert. A dirt road which is passable by passenger car leads to the center of Wyatt's old claims. The distance is about one mile. We scoured the area for old tin cans and other camping and mining equipment as souvenirs of our visit. It has been reported that others have done the same thing, However, Wyatt's claims covered hundreds of acres and there are undoubtedly other mining artifacts from Wyatt's activities to be found in surrounding gullies. We took extensive photographs of the area.

Wyatt and Josie spent over twenty years working these claims in the winter, when the weather in the desert is usually perfect. Wyatt and his friends did considerable underground work, driving several shafts to a depth of probably a hundred feet or more. There are other shallow diggings through out surrounding hills.

The following is a story that shows that Wyatt occasionally slipped away from Josie and his mine to hit town for a little socializing. This article appeared in the *Needles Desert Star* on July 6, 1988, *The Day a Needles Resident Tangled with Gunslinger Wyatt Earp.*[52]

> "Here is a story that you will never see on television, although it involves a personality that is played on television quite regularly — the world's most famous gunslinger, Wyatt Earp. It is a true story which has been told before but bears repeating at this time.
>
> Along about 1910, Earp was in Needles doing nothing except sightseeing and visiting the

saloons and bars. He wasn't wearing his guns because this trip to Needles was just for pleasure.

As the day wore on he was feeling no pain as he ambled along the sidewalk near Williams Jewelry Store. Mr. Williams was out on the walk getting some air and spoke a friendly greeting to the man of the fast draw, not knowing who he was. Earp returned the greeting with such a loud profanity and created such a ruckus that William's son Alfred came out of the store to tell Earp he was disturbing his patrons and if he didn't desist, he would throw him into the street.

Earp ambled off down the street and it seemed the incident was over, but later in the day as Alfred was closing the store, he came back. He asked Alfred if he was the man who going to throw him into the street. Alfred tried to pass off his earlier threats by saying it might have been his brother.

Earp didn't believe this for a moment and after a few more words the two started to tangle. Earp landed in the street with Alfred right on top of him when spectators separated them.

Alfred later said that Earp was quite a street fighter and made quite an effort to do him in. He also said that if he had known the man he had thrown into the street was the most notorious gunman in the West, he would have been scared to death." End of news article.

This is atypical behavior for Wyatt, as he was seldom known to drink much. He was 62 years of age at the time of this incident and there is some reason to believe he drank more as he aged.

Wyatt also built a small frame house for Josie at the little hamlet called Vidal, which is a seven miles south of Vidal Junction. My brother and I located and photographed this old structure. This little house could be the only home that Wyatt and Josie owned during their almost fifty year marriage. Today, Vidal looks to be a ghost town. Perhaps three families live here and the old service stations and cafes are falling apart and covered with graffiti.

Wyatt was honored years ago by the Post Office Department which named a small stop in the road, Earp, California. This little hamlet is located about a mile from Parker, Arizona and is situated almost on the river. The current postmaster is a Wyatt Earp fan. He has photos and other memorabilia of Wyatt on his bulletin board. He keeps a supply of Wyatt Earp stamps and postcards for purchase as souvenirs. He will also provide directions to Wyatt's mine.

This mining venture of Wyatt's, covering over twenty years, says a lot about the man. In San Diego, Wyatt always kept a relatively low profile. This is also true of his mining activity. Josie apparently was quite content with this camping-out style of life. From all indications, the couple were happy and content. Neither sought publicity nor the limelight. They both worked hard and enjoyed the company of close friends who joined them on the desert. While they never made money at this mining venture, they were happy with each others company.

This photograph shows Don Cilch standing on the exact spot where Wyatt and Josie Earp had their mining camp. Old photographs of their rather primitive tent camp show the two distinctive rocks on the horizon at the extreme right. Collection of the authors.

This photograph shows Herb and Ken Cilch, Sr., standing next to a claim location marker on one of Wyatt's claims. This is a new mining claim filed in 1996 and covers one of the old Earp claims. These claims are located almost halfway between Vidal Junction and the Post Office at Earp, California. Collection of the authors.

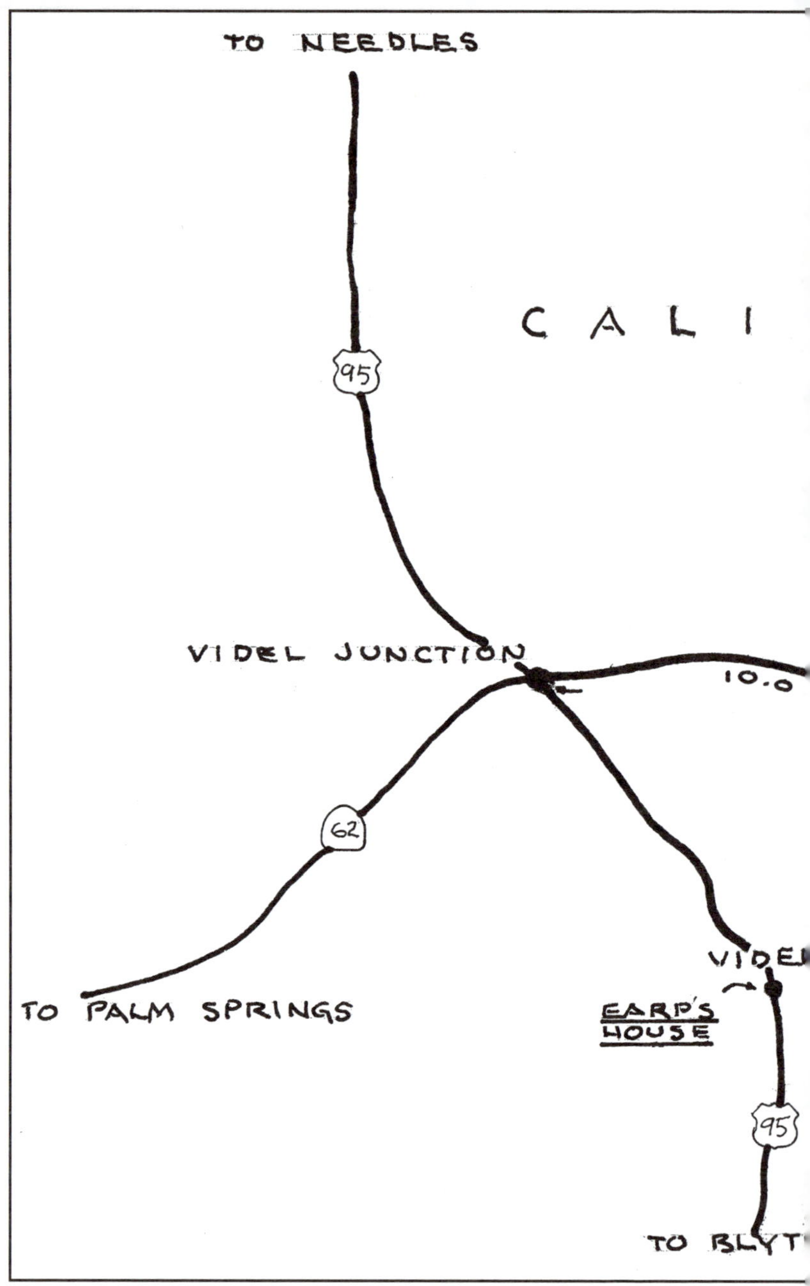

This map shows the location of Wyatt Earp's mining claims on the California desert, the town of Vidal where he and Josie lived and the US Post Office named for Wyatt at Earp, California. He and Josie worked these claims from about 1905 to his death in 1929.

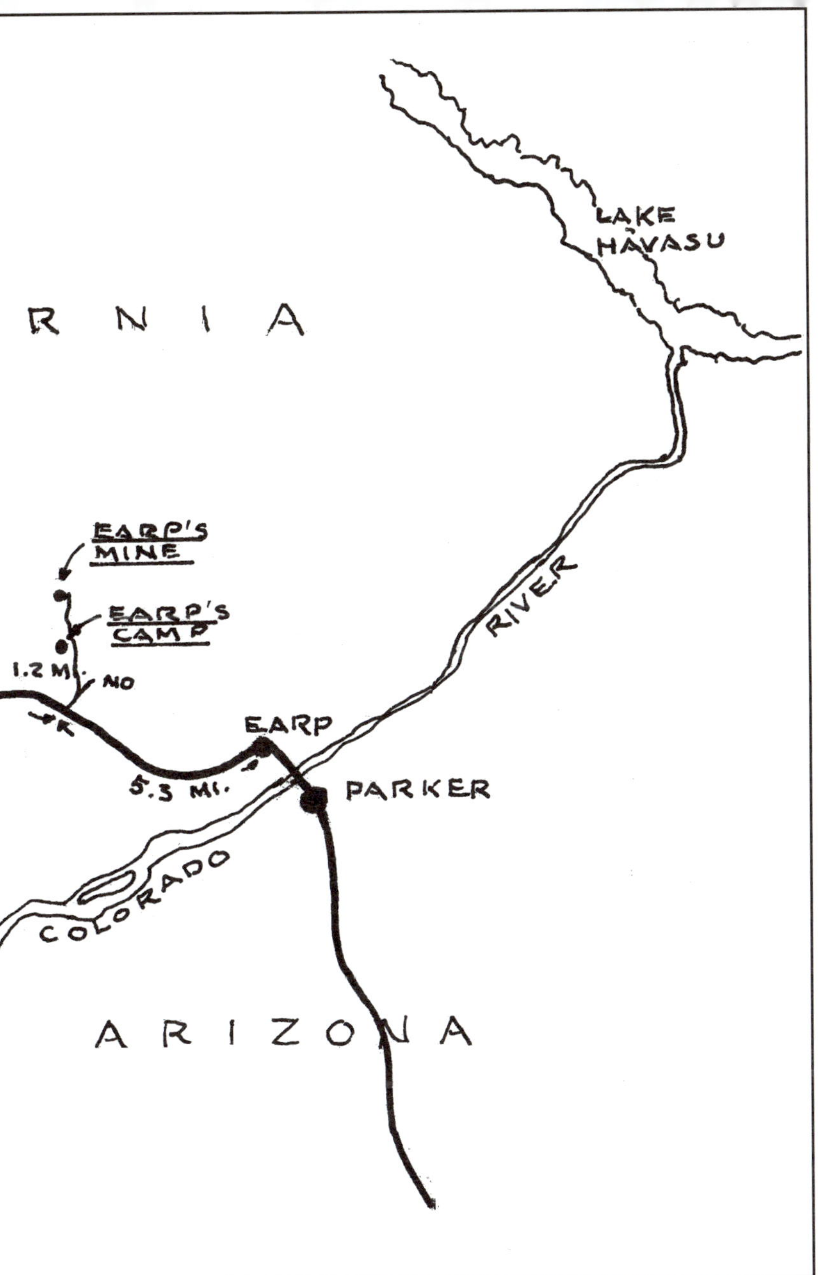

The claims are located on Federal lands administered by the Bureau of Land Management and are open to the public. However, some of the claims have been recently relocated and property rights must be observed. It is recommended that the Earp Post Office be visited as the Postmaster is a friendly and informative Earp fan. Map courtesy Jerry Sullivan.

Chapter Nine
WYATT IN HOLLYWOOD

While Wyatt and Josie's winters were spent mining in the desert, their summers were spent enjoying the California sun. Their lifestyle was modest as they rented a succession of small bungalows in the general Los Angeles area. It is doubtful that they had any kind of steady income. Wyatt has been pictured by some as being easy with his money. He loaned money to friends, grub-staked prospectors and lost more gambling. He undoubtedly sank much of his savings into his own unprofitable mining ventures. Some have speculated that they were helped financially in their later years by Josie's well-to-do relatives.

In time, Wyatt was drawn to the infant motion picture industry that employed many old cowboys in their early Westerns. He is reported to have spent time discussing with them the old days at Dodge City and Tombstone. Many of these old timers either knew Wyatt or had heard of him. While Wyatt was not a household name in those days, he was known to many. As early as the 1870s Wyatt's name was frequently mentioned in newspapers. When any of the Earp boys visited a city a newspaper article would chronicle their arrival. The incident of the OK Corral received almost front page coverage throughout the West.

Wyatt probably was hoping that he could become a consultant in the movies or that someone would pay him for his life story. He attracted notice of the famous silent movie western stars, William S. Hart and Tom Mix. Both of these stars became close friends of Wyatt and tried to get the movie studios to do a film on Wyatt's life. However, the studio heads had no interest.

Historian Paul A. Hutton has researched Wyatt's impact on Hollywood in his often quoted magazine article entitled *Celluloid Lawman or Wyatt Earp Goes to Hollywood*.53 By this time, Wyatt was in his seventies. Dr. Hutton reports that Wyatt did get in the movies, but only as an extra in Douglas Fairbank's film *The Half Breed*. Hutton also tells the story of the young prop boy John Ford interviewing Wyatt about the Old West. He apparently liked Wyatt and plied him with coffee. Ford, later in his *My Darling Clementine* with Henry Fonda, shot the OK Corral scene as Wyatt had described it. This is judged to be the best of the early Earp films.

Hutton reveals in his article that Bat Masterson, then a newspaperman in New York and friend of Theodore Roosevelt, first introduced Stuart Lake to Wyatt's history. As an aside, Bat Masterson was a sportswriter in New York and palled around with Stuart Lake and Damon Runyon. Runyon is alleged to have patterned the character of Sky Masterson in *Guys and Dolls* after Bat. An amusing anecdotal story concerning Bat was told to the author when he was a boy by his father, Col. J.H. Cilch. My father met Bat in New York City after attending an Adventure Club meeting with the author Rex Beach. The story follows: Bat was continually badgered by acquaintances who wanted him to give them his personal gun that he carried at Dodge City. So Bat made a practice of visiting pawn shops in the New York area and buying older, reasonably priced Colt revolvers similar to the ones carried by lawmen in the West. He would then, after wrapping the handle with black tape and with great fanfare, present the gun to a friend. Everyone was happy.

Bat Masterson also led a colorful and adventurous life.54 He was five years younger than Wyatt, born in 1853. He was described as being handsome, gregarious and with a good sense of humor. He was well known as a fearless law officer and gained fame from his involvement in the battle of Adobe Walls, Texas, where 28 hunters held off a force of 500 Comanches, Kiowas and Cheyennes. He was also involved in several notorious shootouts. He eventually moved to New York City where President Theodore Roosevelt appointed him US Marshal for the Southern district of New York. He later worked as a sportswriter for the New York

Morning Telegraph. He died at his sports desk on October 25, 1921. Another unknown New York paper wrote, " He died at his desk, gripping his pen with the tenacity with which he clung to his six shooter." His last written words were, " There are many in this old world of ours who hold that things break about even for all of us. I have observed for example that we all get about the same amount of ice. The rich get it in the summer and the poor get it in the winter." My friend, former State Senator Hugo Fisher, also related this story to me and he may have heard it from his friend Stuart Lake.

Lake was a press secretary for Teddy Roosevelt and a western frontier buff. After interviewing Bat about Wyatt, he then came West to interview the famous lawman. Unfortunately, Lake did not interview Wyatt until he was almost 80 years of age and a bit infirm. His biography, *Wyatt Earp Frontier Marshal*, published two years after Wyatt's death, was a sensation.[55] It became a best seller and was serialized in *Saturday Evening Post*. Lake continued by writing a series of short stories and screen plays on Wyatt. It's a shame that Wyatt couldn't have lived to see the stir that he created. From then to now there has been a never-ending series of books and films based on his life.

Stuart Lake died in San Diego on January 27, 1964. His obituary written by Charles Hull which appeared in the *San Diego Union*, revealed details of his interesting life.[56] He was born in Rome, New York in 1889. After graduating from Cornell University he became a newspaper correspondent in the Far East. He returned home to work on the *New York Herald.* With war clouds looming over Europe, he joined Theodore Roosevelt's writing staff. With the outbreak of war, he entered the military and was sent to France. He was wounded in action and walked with a limp the rest of his life. He was in an Army hospital for three years after the war. He also earned the Silver Star. Stuart was a true war hero. He later came to San Diego for health reasons and remained for the rest of his life.

Alfred JaCoby, an editor of the *San Diego Union*, relates a story in an article dated October 10, 1960 as to how Stuart hooked up with Wyatt in Hollywood.57 In this article, entitled *The Life and Legend of Stuart Lake,* he relates the following story,

> "Early in 1925 while working in Hollywood, Lake actually mentioned on a movie set that he had been trying to find information about Earp, 'but no one knows even where or when he died.' That was on a Friday. The following Monday, a workman on the set told Lake, 'I've got a message for you. Call Wyatt Earp.'

> The workman told how he had visited in Long Beach over the weekend and had met an old man and his wife who were introduced as Mr. and Mrs. Earp.

> 'Any relation to Wyatt,' he asked? I am Wyatt Earp, the old man answered. Lake's interest had been passed on. Of course, Lake did call Wyatt."

Photograph of Col. J.H. Cilch, mine owner, civil and mining engineer, explorer and soldier of fortune. He spent most of his career in South and Central America. He knew Bat Masterson in New York. The American outlaws Butch Cassidy and the Sundance Kid worked under his supervision at the Concordia Tin Mine in Bolivia. Collection of the authors.

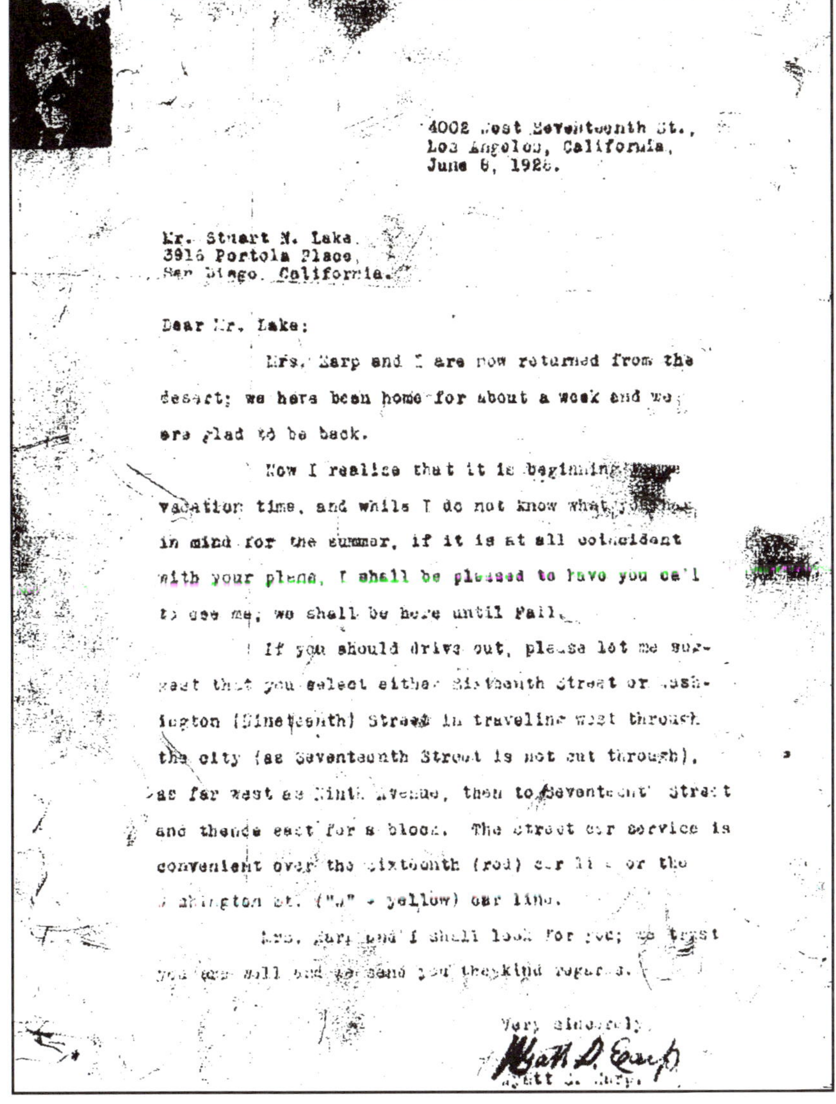

This copy of a letter, dated June 8, 1928, is written and signed by Wyatt Earp to Stuart Lake. The letter is an invitation to visit Josie and Wyatt and gives thorough directions to the Earp's residence in Los Angeles. This letter may have set the stage for their first meeting and could be the genesis for Lake's best selling book, "Wyatt Earp, Frontier Marshal" and the subsequent Earp myth. Collection of the authors.

Chapter Ten

STUART LAKE INTERVIEWS

Wyatt Earp's biographer, Stuart Lake, was interviewed by an unknown member of the San Diego Historical Society as part of their Oral History Program.[58] The date of the interview is also unknown. This gathering was apparently part of a writers colony in San Diego. The interview is reported in its entirety because Lake seldom gave interviews and he does speak of his meetings with Wyatt.   In opening comments by the questioner, Stuart was congratulated for the great success of his Earp biography *Wyatt Earp Frontier Marshal*. It was pointed out that the book was not only on the best seller list, but used as a textbook in universities all over the country. One chapter in particular is used as a text for descriptive writing at Oxford University, alongside the Gettysburg Address and other classics.

When asked about Wyatt Earp, Lake confirmed he lived in San Diego for a period of time. For that matter he said, " Several prominent San Diego families today owe their economic well-being to the activities around Tombstone, Arizona during Wyatt's time there. When silver was discovered about half of old San Diego went to Tombstone in 1879 and a number made their fortunes with which they returned here.

To get back to Earp, he, of course, had already made his reputation as a frontier marshal at Dodge City and Wichita. He went to Tombstone, not as a peace officer, but to establish a stage line. The camp was pretty wild then with a lawless tough bunch. There were the Clantons, who were running the town and refusing to pay taxes, which was the sheriff's job to collect in those days.

As Wyatt went through Tucson, he was told that there already were two stage lines in Tombstone and that maybe he'd be better off at his old trade. So he accepted a deputy sheriff's commission taking law and order into Tombstone. Later he was made a deputy United States Marshal."

Question: "When did he come to San Diego?" Answer: "The Tombstone boom collapsed in 1883 when the mines struck an underground river down at the 600 foot level. It became a ghost town. After some time in Colorado and Idaho Wyatt came to San Diego. That was about 1886."

Question: "What brought him here?" Answer: "Well, the same thing that brought thousands of others. San Diego was a boom town: there was lots of money to be made here. There were some stakes and some mining excitement up around Descanso. It was also a wide open town. Wyatt operated the three biggest gambling houses in San Diego; one on 4th Street across from the Plaza and a couple of others down around 6th Street. He bought a lot of property here, including a block in the Hillcrest area on University between 4th and 5th; some on University and Washington. He owned property at 4th and Cedar; several blocks on India Street; all over town. Incidentally, he had a string of harness horses that he raced. He also competed at the race track that was on the flats across the highway at about where the Brown Military Academy is now."

Question: "How long did Wyatt stay in San Diego?" Answer: "Until about 1888, as long as the money was rolling in. He did make quite a lot of money while he was here, too. When the San Diego boom burst he left. He gave away some of his real estate and he let the rest go for taxes.

Of course, then it was mostly wilderness: sagebrush, cactus, jack rabbits. Today it is worth hundreds of thousands of dollars. For one example, that Hillcrest block I mentioned Wyatt gave away to a widow of a man who had worked for him at one time."

Question: "I suppose you got to know Wyatt Earp pretty well yourself while gathering material for your biography?" Answer: "Yes. I spent a lot of time with him during the six years I was getting material for this book. He was living in Los Angeles at the time and he used to come down here and stay for several weeks. And I'd go to Los Angeles and talk to him a good deal about the old days in the West. Two days before he died in 1929, when he was 80 years old, we were all packed and ready to go to the desert where we were going to do some more talking. On Friday, he telephoned that he wasn't feeling well and we'd better postpone the trip."

Question: "Why did you pick Wyatt Earp as the subject of a biography that took so many years of constant work?" Answer: " I found in him the perfect type specimen of a frontier law enforcement officer. Wyatt wasn't the most conspicuous sort of a person: a circus type, a Buffalo Bill kind of hero, but he was genuine and his reputation wasn't based on doubtful legend. There are many so-called heroes of the old west like Wild Bill Hickok or Billy the Kid who actually were cold-blooded killers. They never gave the other fellow an even break.

In the 1870s when the West was being developed these legends were easy to perpetuate. Like the one about Wild Bill Hickok single-handedly wiped out the so-called McCandless Gang. This story ran in the old Harper's Magazine and was written by a man who was a notorious faker. The legend took hold and in most cases of this kind it is the legend that has remained in the public's mind. The truth would have had a hard, hard time. Wild Bill Hickok's myth was exploded long ago by the Nebraska State Historical Association. Other reliable authorities have taken it apart. Nevertheless, it still prevails."

Question: "That is interesting, Stu, now let's get down to one of your other well known stories, *Vinegar Joe and the Jersey Lily*, from which the motion picture, *The Westerner*, was made. What Western figure was the hero of that story?" Answer: "That is the story of Judge Roy Bean of Texas. Incidentally, Judge Roy was in San Diego at one time and he was at our first jail down here in Old Town right at the close of the Mexican War. As far as his story is concerned, I guess I am the only one who knows that he passed these laws and took them to jail.

Whether it is fact or fiction I try to keep my stuff authentic. I've spent the last twenty-five years hunting out old guys with long white whiskers who were a part of the old west. I'd get their stories and then I'd check them and recheck them against old records and obvious sources. I do this because their memories are actually faulty or they are stringing facts.

Question: "How did you ever get into the writing game?" Answer: "I started writing when I was at Cornell University. I corresponded with a couple of New York papers and I worked at the *Coronado Sun* which was the only morning daily at that time in the town of Ithaca, New York."

Question: "After college did you go to work on a paper full time?" Answer: "Yes, I worked in New York, Seattle, San Francisco. I went to the Orient with the Associated Press. After a couple of years there I returned to New York and went on the staff with James Gordon Bennett at the old *New York Herald*."

Question" " What sort of assignments did you have?" Answer: "I wrote baseball, I did politics, I did everything - an all-around newspaper reporter for the paper."

Question: "Did you do much free lance writing at that time?" Answer: "I started writing pulp as far back as 1912. I adapted several stage plays for the screen. I wrote for one hundred dollars a script for Louis Selznick. He was the father of David Selznick who is now one of the more important producers in Hollywood. Those were the days of Clara Kimball Young, Herbert Flynn, Robert Morley, Nazimova and other stars of the day.

Then the First World War started and I was press agent for Colonel Theodore Roosevelt, a PR man and I prepared some of his speeches. I had become acquainted with Roosevelt during his 1912 Bull Moose campaign. He was always a fanatic about adequate security and disposition before World War I. I helped him try to put across his messages."

Question: "And how did you finally land in San Diego?" Answer: "After I had gone back to France a fellow in an army hospital there told me about San Diego and that it was a nice place in which to live, that it was an easy place to live and get around in. So I came here and continued writing."

Question: "Was it after you came to San Diego that you began to specialize in Western lives and Western historical writing?" Answer: "I guess you might say so. I'd been doing quite a lot of stuff for the *Saturday Evening Post*. I did a series on hunting, buffalo hunters, cows and cow towns. I came out with one called *Straight Shooting Guys* and another one which was half fact and half fiction about the old Texas Rangers. People seem to like them so others followed."

Question: "And what are you working on now?" Answer: "I've just finished a script for Walter Wanger which I called *Winchester 73*. It is a story of that famous rifleman. This story is built around a particular rifle of that model. It tells what happened to various people who owned one at one time or another."

"Thanks, Stuart Lake, for this fascinating inside story of one of San Diego's most successful authors." End of interview.

Over the years some of the biggest names in Hollywood have portrayed Wyatt in film in on television. Some of the earlier stars were Walter Houston, Randolph Scott, Johnny Mack Brown and Richard Dix. Of more recent vintage were Henry Fonda (twice), Ronald Reagan, Burt Lancaster, James Garner, Kevin Costner and

Kurt Russell. On television the long running *The Life and Legend of Wyatt Earp* was played by Hugh O'Brien. Equally long running was *Gunsmoke* with James Arness. The Arness character, Matt Dillon, was supposedly patterned after Wyatt. This exposure has firmly fixed Wyatt's "good guy" image in the public's mind.

Lake's book was quite well written and captured the interest of all Western buffs.59 Unfortunately, without Wyatt to edit the final version, Lake portrayed Wyatt as a knight in shining armor. He apparently relied too much on word of mouth accounts of Wyatt's alleged adventures. The book, although very well written, has been criticized as exaggerating Wyatt's exploits. Other writers have gone the other way and attempted to portray Wyatt and his brothers as crooks. Hutton, the historian, describes an alleged quote by a Hollywood director, to wit, "Wyatt Earp was crooked as a three dollar bill. He and his brothers were racketeers. They shook people down and they did everything they could to get dough."60 There is no written proof that any of these allegations are true. Part of the problem is that some individuals are being politically correct in that they apply today's standards to the America's wild West. Gambling and saloon ownership were respectable occupations in those times. It was expected that saloon owners would employ dancehall girls and whores. In most mining camps the red light ladies were the only females within a hundred miles. Their services were needed and appreciated by all frontier men.

Lake, in his book on Wyatt, is quoted as follows, "More than any other man of record in his time he represents the exact combination of breeding and human experience which laid the foundations of Western empire."61 This statement could probably apply to his brothers Virgil and Morgan as well. Virgil actually had a more distinguished law enforcement career than Wyatt.

The Earp family were true pioneers and contributed significantly to the development of America's western frontier. Thomas, the first Earp to arrive in this country in the early 1700s, produced offspring who fought in the American Revolution. Prior to the Civil War the Earps resided in North Carolina, Tennessee and Kentucky. Most were farmers and a few were preachers and teachers. Nicholas Earp, father of Wyatt and his brothers, was born in North Carolina in 1813. He married Wyatt's mother, Virginia Ann Cooksey, in 1840. Nicholas had a prior marriage that produced a son, Newton. Their other children were James, born in 1841; Virgil, born in 1843; sister Martha born in 1845; Wyatt born in 1848; Morgan born in 1851; Warren, born in 1855 and another sister, Virginia, born in 1858.

Nicholas Earp was primarily a farmer, but was involved in local politics. He served as part time constable, notary public and justice of the peace. He served as a sergeant in the Mexican War and received a lifetime pension for injuries suffered in this engagement. He named Wyatt after his commanding officer, Captain Wyatt Berry Stapp. Nicholas was granted a land grant of 160 acres for his Mexican War service near Pella, Iowa. He moved his family from Monmouth, Illinois, where Wyatt was born, to Pella, Iowa in 1850.

At the outbreak of the Civil War, Nicholas was involved in the forming of several regiments in his area. For his efforts, he was appointed deputy US Provost Marshal in his area. Three of his sons, Newton, Virgil and James, all enlisted in the Union forces and served more than two years in combat regiments.

In 1864 Nicholas convinced residents of Pella that he had been in the California gold fields in 1851. On this basis he was appointed wagonmaster and led a train of forty wagons successfully to California. It has been said that he did not lose one person.

Within a few years Nicholas returned to the midwest with his family and later led another wagon train west. It was at this time that Wyatt married and lost his wife in childbirth and disappeared into Kansas where he, among other things, apparently was involved in the buffalo hide business. Virgil and his wife Allie were part of this wagon train, but dropped off at Prescott, Arizona Territory, where Virgil drove wagons and became involved in law enforcement.

Nicholas then settled in the Colton, Redlands area, near San Bernardino, California. The family remained there for many years. This became the family home. Morgan and his mother are buried in a local cemetery. Nicholas died at an old soldiers home nearby and may be buried there. Virgil was chief of police of Colton for a number of years and his father was again involved in politics and served as a justice of the peace. There are a number of Earp relatives still in the area.

The Earp family traveled extensively throughout the western frontier; much more than most pioneer families. Their presence was felt wherever they lived. The public's perception of the old West has been influenced by their activities and the way it has been portrayed in the media.

Chapter Eleven
TRAIL'S END

After a short illness Wyatt Earp died in his sleep on January 13, 1929, in Los Angeles at age 80. According to Josie his last visitor was his old friend John Clum. His death was reported in most newspapers across the country. Josie was too heartbroken to attend the funeral.

The following press release, by the *Los Angeles Times* was dated January 17, 1929 with this heading and story, *Earp Buried by the Old West, Pioneer Folk Gather at Rites of Peace Officer Whose Life Molded Frontier History.*[62]

Wyatt Earp's funeral was conducted down at Pierce Brothers Chapel yesterday and it was like a reunion of the sturdy men and women who knew Wyatt as a wiry six foot two gun officer of the law in mining town, cowcamps and almost anywhere along the frontier where trouble was apt to pop loose.

George M. Easton came in from Colton, a lawman who helped clean up that town at a time when outlawry was so rampant that desperadoes used to ride into town at night and knock out the lamps in houses with their guns. Cowboy actor Bill (William S.) Hart, no novice in the ways of the West himself, came in from his place and was one of the pallbearers. Bill as a little boy knew Wyatt in Dodge City when that town was going good on the frontier. Actor Tom Mix was there and as a friend of the deceased was a pall bearer.

There was a Mrs. Roma Thoirndyke, widow of Melburn Thoirndyke, who was numbered among the mourners. Tears filled her eyes as she told how she remembered as a child of seven years of age back there in Tombstone in 1881, the day that Wyatt shot it out with the Clantons. As a child would, she ran out into the street the minute she heard the shooting start. But someone grabbed her and threw her onto the floor in a grocery store or something. Maj. John P. Clum was a long time friend of the Earps. He was the very first mayor of Tombstone and Wyatt Earp was his first chief of police.

The Mayor was founder and editor of the *Tombstone Epitaph*, a newspaper that is wrapped in history of the southwest and is still reporting the doings of Tombstone and surrounding territories. That was in 1881. Major Clum and Wyatt's trail crossed again up in the Yukon territory in 1898 and in Nome, Alaska in 1900. The Major was extending the Postal service in Alaska at that time and Wyatt was gold hunting.

Wilson Mizner, another pallbearer and J.P. Browner knew Earp up in the Klondike Country. Also they met Major Clum again for the first time since then at the funeral yesterday. Other pallbearers included George W. Parsons, formerly of Tombstone, Charles Welch, Fred Dornberger and Jim Mitchell.

Many Assemble

Out from the colorful past of the old West, stepped these friends of Wyatt Earp. Their numbers increased by others until extra chairs had to be brought into the chapel to seat them all.
There they sat these colorful company of

This is another photograph of Wyatt taken shortly before his death in 1929. He is sitting on the railing of his porch in Los Angeles The address of this residence is believed to be 4002 West Seventeenth Street, Los Angeles. Ca. Courtesy Arizona Historical Society, Tucson, Az., Photo ID # 76618.

Here we see Wyatt posed with a shiny new car. This photograph was probably taken in Los Angeles. The car must have belonged to a friend as there is no record of Wyatt or Josie ever owning a motor vehicle. Courtesy Arizona Historical Society, Tucson, Az., Photo ID # 76624.

This view of Wyatt shows him standing on the porch of Josie's and his small rented house in Los Angeles in the late 1920s. Courtesy Arizona Historical Society, Tucson, Az., Photo ID # 76622.

Here we see Wyatt informally resting in his armchair. This photograph was taken shortly before his death in 1929. He apparently never smiled for a photograph. Courtesy Arizona Historical Society, Tucson, Az., Photo ID # 76623.

actors from the melodrama of the older days. Bronzed of face and those who were not white haired were bald headed. Many of them carried canes and they were not for mere ornaments either. Some wore business suits and some wore heavy jackets of wool or leather: some with large long overcoats made to turn the wind that has a habit of driving the chill into the bones when one is getting old. There was a sprinkling of younger folks there too.

All were sitting there in the chapel before Wyatt's bier banked high with flowers while somewhere came the music of a harp. These men and women no doubt let their thoughts drift back to the unhappy turbulent days when the man in the casket there before them was among them helping to lay the foundations for the west of today.

When Doctor Harper of the Wilshire Boulevard Congregational Church began to speak these veterans snapped out of the reverie and leaned forward.

Some of them rested their elbows on their canes as they cupped their hands over their ears.

Man of the Plains

We are here to pay our respects to one who has journeyed across the plains of life for a long time, said Dr. Harper, Yea! Most of those before him knew just what that journey meant.

One ruddy faced neighbor of old eased in through the door and dropped into a seat in the back row. He wore a pink carnation in his lapel. He meant to be quiet but when he was settling down he recognized the man next to him, as one he had not seen in years and slapped him on the shoulder and said quite audibly, well!! old timer how are you? They mumbled along during most of the sermon apparently swapping comments. The brief service over, the mourners passed by the coffin and as they came out through the side door there were plenty whose eyes were red . Among those who were present, were Tom Grady, M.C. Beckwith, Dr. D.K. Dickinson, who knew Earp in Tombstone many years ago; Jack Cochrane, who knew him in Alaska, George B. Calnan who knew him in El Paso; Joe Treest who knew him in Tonopah and Goldfield; E.A. Speegle of Tombstone Days, and Frank E. Cline a friend of his for the past twenty years in Los Angeles." End of news article.

The Los Angeles Times also ran a photograph of the pall bearers standing outside the chapel. There is rumored to be another photograph showing Tom Mix standing next to the coffin with his cowboy hat held over his heart.

Wyatt's remains were cremated. Josie has described her heartbroken train ride to San Francisco, cradling an urn with Wyatt's ashes in her arms.63 Her beloved husband was buried at her parents' plot at a Colma, California cemetery, just south of San Francisco. Josie was buried in the same plot after her death in 1944, at age 75.

This portrait of Wyatt is dated 1928 at an unknown location. Wyatt was 79 years of age at this time and he looks like a banker or minister. Clearly, at this advanced age, he was still a man to be reckoned with. Courtesy Arizona Historical Society, Tucson, Az., Photo ID # 1448.

Chapter Twelve
SUMMING UP

There is compelling evidence that Wyatt Earp in many ways stood apart from his frontier contemporaries. His courage and fearlessness as well as his self confidence and singleness of purpose have been attested to by many sources. The author recently ran across an oral interview with Henry H. Weddle who was an old time Immigration Officer in San Diego. This is another interview conducted and recorded by the San Diego Historical Society.64 In his interview Weddle indicated he knew Wyatt as they both raced quarterhorses at Tijuana. He relates one instance where he followed Wyatt into a saloon filled with Mexicans. As Wyatt walked in the Mexicans parted for him like he was royalty. They couldn't have known who Wyatt was or anything about his reputation. He just had a determined look about him. This incident confirms other accounts of how Wyatt could influence groups of men merely by his presence.

Wyatt was an imposing-looking man, even in old age. Photographs of him in his late seventies reveal a man still to be reckoned with. He could have passed as a stern minister or banker.

Critics have characterized Wyatt as a womanizer. While he may have been inclined in this direction, Josie curtailed any real liaisons. She was jealous of her husband and kept a close eye on him. She was also very protective of Wyatt. She cared deeply for him. This is demonstrated by her sticking with him throughout his nomadic travels to mining camps extending over almost a half a century.

Peace officers in Wichita and Dodge City have attested to his self confidence and lack of fear. Doc Holliday, himself one of the most fearless men in the West, spoke of Wyatt almost in awe. Bat

This is the former grave marker of Wyatt and Josie as seen in 1996 at the Hills of Eternity Memorial Park in Colma, California which is located just south of San Francisco. Unfortunately, vandals keep stealing the grave stones. A friend has recently informed us that the above marker was partially defaced and was replaced. Collection of the authors.

This is the cemetery plot where Wyatt and Josie are interred. It is located at the Hills of Eternity Memorial Park, 1301 El Camino Real, Colma, Ca. The imposing grave marker is new. Over the years vandals and thieves have taken or defaced previous markers. Cemetery officials report that fifteen to twenty visitors a week request directions to the gravesite. Photograph courtesy Jimmy Trent Bradshaw.

Masterson was quoted on several occasions regarding Wyatt's mastery over men.

On Thursday, October 2,1972, Don Freeman, columnist for the *San Diego Union*, discussed in an interesting article Wyatt's place in history.[65] He posed this question to John Gilchriese, historian at the University of Arizona and a student of the Earp saga for over thirty years. "Was Wyatt Earp a hero?"

"Heroes are made in Hollywood," replied Gilchriese. "I doubt if Wyatt Earp considered himself a hero. Hundreds of peace officers in the West did the same thing as Wyatt every day."

"Wyatt Earp," said Gilchriese, "was a product of his time, a businessman who often wore a badge, a frontier gambler-as many men were-and a man of tremendous nerve. He was taciturn, withdrawn man. He had an aura of mystery about him and he became a symbol of the West. But all of the films about him have been over-romanticized, misleading and inaccurate."

The following quote will present another side of a complex man. Here Wyatt is discussing the shootout at the OK Corral,

> "There are more corpses in Hamlet than there was in the OK Corral and with less reason. We didn't kill none of the wrong men like Hamlet done to poor Polonius. He was a talkative man and wouldn't have lasted long in Kansas. The men we killed there had to be killed. They were bad and if any part of the country lets itself be stampeded by bad men, it will infect the whole shebang before it's through. That fight didn't take but about 30 seconds and it seems like, in my going on 80 years, we could find some other happenings to discuss." [66]

Wyatt had significant impact on most communities in which he lived. At Wichita and Dodge, Kansas and Tombstone, Arizona, he was known for his law enforcement roles. Here he was most noted for his fearlessness and determination. At San Diego, California, Nome, Alaska and Tonopah, Nevada, he was respected for his business acumen. While in San Diego he accumulated a small fortune and controlled gambling in Tijuana, Mexico. His saloon in Tonopah, Nevada was very profitable. He also appears to have operated the most successful saloon in Nome.

Another interesting facet of Wyatt's life was his ability to sustain life long friendships. If he was dishonest or a confidence man as some have alleged, he would not have been revered by such diverse individuals as Doc Holliday, Bat Masterson, Lucky Baldwin, John Clum, and others. John Clum, in particular, enjoyed a distinguished career, virtually without blemish. His friendship and loyalty to Wyatt spanned almost fifty years. These friendships, combined with the large turnout and sentiments expressed at Wyatt's funeral, speak for themselves.

Another respected friend of many years was Fred Dodge, an undercover agent of Wells Fargo and a lawman of note, for most of his career His diaries and memoirs were edited by Stuart Lake's daughter Carolyn Lake in her book, *Fred Dodge, Undercover for Wells Fargo, The Unvarnished Recollections Of,* published in 1969.[67]

These recollections include a series of letters exchanged between Wyatt, Stuart Lake and Dodge and reveal the great respect that the Wells Fargo man had for both Wyatt and Lake. It should be noted that Dodge was appointed an undercover agent by John J. Valentine, President of Wells Fargo. In one of these letters, Lake asked Dodge what he thought of Wyatt as a man and peace officer. Dodge replied that "as a man he was Ace high and as a peace officer he was Peace." He went on, " I never knew Wyatt to be other than quiet, cool and courageous. His head was always clear, which showed he was absolutely devoid of fear."

In another letter from Fred Dodge to Stuart Lake dated October 26, 1931, he congratulates Lake on his Earp book and states, " you have drawn an accurate picture of one of the coolest and bravest men I have ever known." Fred's admiration of Wyatt as a man and peace officer is repeated time after time. This is high praise from another peace officer of that era.

The following obituary of Fred Dodge appeared in the *Boerne Texas Star* of November 22, 1938,

> "Fred Dodge died on November 16, 1938.[68] He was 84 and one of the last surviving peace officers of the frontier where he had been cool, quiet and a dead shot and where his native ability as a detective was widely known and respected. His keen sense of justice made him so square with all men, even lawbreakers that many times those who had served out their time turned to him for help in getting a new start in life. With his inheritance of pioneer resourcefulness, innate wisdom and quiet courage, Fred Dodge, his modesty notwithstanding, made a place for himself in the history of law enforcement and in the history of his country."

The above and previous testimonials attesting to Wyatt Earp's character and role as a peace officer should help to diminish various authors claims of criminal and unethical behavior on his part. It is true that he was arrested as a youth for alleged horse theft and later in life on a crooked gambling charge but he was never convicted. He was arrested and fined in San Francisco for carrying a concealed weapon into the ring of the Sharkey-Fitzsimmons heavyweight fight. Does this constitute questionable behavior or morals in a frontier environment?

Wyatt's taking the law into his own hands after the wounding of Virgil and the murder of Morgan is another matter. Under the color of authority Wyatt hunted and killed his brothers assassins. If you were related to the men killed at the OK Corral or Frank Stilwell and the other assailants, it would be understandable if you harbored ill feelings. However, many other observers applauded Wyatt's actions. It is noteworthy that the governor of Colorado refused to extradite Wyatt on murder charges drummed up by Sheriff Behan, Wyatt's enemy. These charges in Arizona were later dismissed completely.

Many fans of the American West are puzzled by the anti-Earp feeling among some authors and especially contemporary residents of Tombstone, Arizona. It must be remembered that merchants and miners friendly to the Earp faction left Tombstone after the mines failed. The cowboys and rustlers and some of their descendants remain in the Tombstone area.

It should also be emphasized that Fred Dodge read and approved of Stuart Lake's book on Wyatt's life. Dodge was an important and knowledgable figure in the Tombstone-OK Corral saga. There is no known reason why he might have been unduly biased toward Wyatt. He apparently approved of Wyatt's actions in Tombstone.

In his undercover role in Tombstone, Fred Dodge was able to uncover many fascinating items. For instance, his memoirs revealed that Ike Clanton and others told him that Wyatt did kill Curley Bill and that Doc Holliday was a participant in a stagecoach robbery. He further stated that Sheriff Behan appointed Frank Stilwell a deputy sheriff knowing he was a stage robber. As you may remember, Frank Stilwell, with companions, murdered Morgan Earp.

For serious Wyatt Earp fans, Richard E. Erwin's book, *The Truth About Wyatt Earp,* is must reading.69 His chapter on *Creators and Debunkers of the Wyatt Earp Myth,* clearly delineates between Wyatt supporters and detractors. He categorizes Earp writers as either myth makers, Earp bashers or those who told the story to the best of their ability. We hope that our book falls in the latter category.

Summing up, Wyatt Earp was a remarkable and gifted man who led a remarkable life. He was admired by almost all of his peers. It has been suggested that his epitaph should read, "Here lies a man." Most of us would agree.

EPILOGUE

The American western frontier was truly a unique period in world history. It holds a special fascination not only for Americans but for peoples from all over the world. This short period of time, perhaps fifty years at best, blended a mixture of discovery, danger, adventure and personal freedom seldom experienced. The wide sweep of the frontier encompassed fur traders, prospectors, miners, Indians (friendly and hostile), soldiers, cowboys, homesteaders, badmen and lawmen. There were no class distinctions. Men and women were judged on their individual accomplishments, good and bad. Mark Twain, in his book *Roughing It*, described an incident that occurred at a stage station somewhere on the frontier.70 One evening, a well-dressed English Lord rode up to the station, dismounted and tossed the reins to a cowboy standing nearby. The cowboy immediately threw the reins back to the aristocratic Englishman and stated, "Either you take care of your horse or you won't eat tonight."

Men like Wyatt Earp and most frontier women were a special breed. Many men and women of today do not measure up to their nineteenth century counterparts.

Life prior to the twentieth century was hard. For the most part men and women worked from dawn to dusk. To survive without social security, welfare and other government aid, people had to be strong and self sufficient. People worked or starved. For this reason families stuck together. Relatives and neighbors helped each other. But for all of the hardships, for the successful ones, there was a silver lining; the attainment of self confidence. People of that harsh era had confidence that they could cope with most of life's travails.

A case in point: When hundreds of wagon trains rolled west

out of Missouri in the mid 1850s, many turned back after only a few days on the trail. This was sufficient time for many to glimpse the hardships that awaited them. This started a weeding-out process that continued throughout the journey.

Those who successfully completed the overland trip were elated and immensely proud of themselves. They had to cope day by day to survive. When a wagon wheel broke the family fixed it. When low on food, someone took a rifle and brought back game. They conquered the fear of the unknown, hostile indians, flooded rivers and all of the hardships associated with traveling over one thousand miles in a covered wagon. For the rest of their lives, they felt a sense of pride and a feeling that nothing was beyond them. Most of all, they had confidence in themselves.

This same phenomenon was observed in the Klondike gold rush. Those hardy individuals who endured the cruel hardships of the Arctic cold to reach the gold fields at Dawson City walked about town with their chests puffed out. It did not matter to many that they arrived too late to become rich. Just reaching Dawson City was the highlight of their lives. They had made it while thousands of others had failed.

Men like Wyatt Earp were a product of their times. Their environment made them strong and self-reliant. Wyatt was successful in his law enforcement career because he was supremely self-confident. He was largely without fear and had a bit of luck. He intimidated many opponents, initially with his demeanor and force of will. He backed this up with his fists and gun. Few men were his equal. Wyatt Earp lives on as a legend, and rightly so.

1 Gaslamp Books and Museum, 413 Market

2 Former Prostitution: Lester Hotel, 417 Market

3 Wyatt Earp Residence: Belle View Rooming House, NE corner 4th & G St.

4 Wyatt Earp Residence: Schmitt Bldg , Rooms, 946 3rd Ave.

5 Wyatt Earp saloon: 951 4th St., now a pawn shop (original bldg.)

6 Wyatt Earp saloon: NW corner of 6 & G St., name unknown

7 Wyatt Earp saloon, Oyster Bar, 837 5th Ave., (upstairs, former prostitution, Golden Poppy Hotel

8 Wyatt Earp saloon, just South of St. James Hotel, on 6th Ave.

9 Former Prositution: Yuma Hotel, 631-635 5th Ave.

10 Former Prositution: Lincoln Hotel, 536 5th Ave.

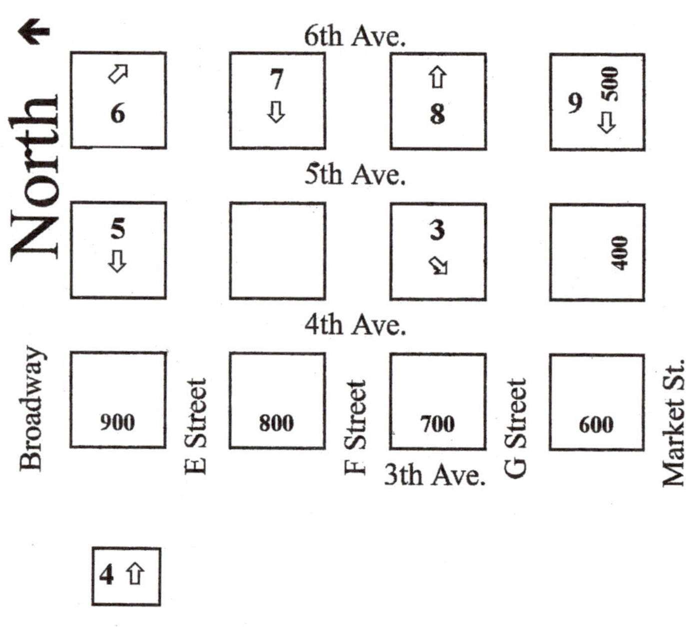

Historic Gaslamp District

MAP

In the Era of Wyatt Earp
Showing the Red Light District
and Wyatt Earp's Hangouts

August 1996

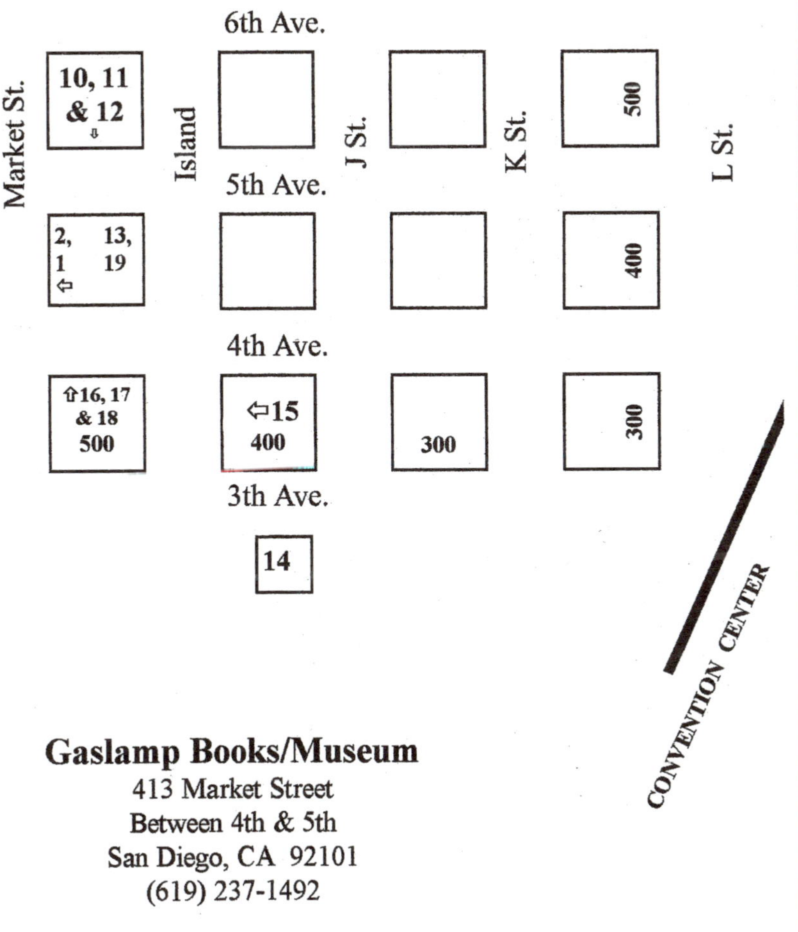

Gaslamp Books/Museum

413 Market Street
Between 4th & 5th
San Diego, CA 92101
(619) 237-1492

MAP-ADDENDUM

For die-hard Wyatt Earp fans, a map of the old Gaslamp/Stingaree District is provided showing Wyatt's haunts. In the 1880s every large city had a Red Light District and San Diego was no exception. This addenda will hopefully give some flavor to this colorful and exciting part of San Diego's history. Come and re-trace Wyatt's steps.

1.   Gaslamp Books and Museum of Historic San Diego which includes the Wyatt Earp Room, 413 Market, between 4th & 5th in downtown San Diego.
2. Prostitution-Lester Hotel, 417 Market, located above Gaslamp Books & Museum. This hotel was raided by police on a regular basis. The thirteenth step on the staircase, when stepped on, sounded an alarm in each room. The girls would slip into an adjoining room by way of a secret panel, thus avoiding arrest. No resident of the hotel ever stepped on number thirteen.
3. Belle View Rooms, NE corner of 4th & G Street. This was one of Wyatt and Josie's first residences in San Diego. The rooms were located upstairs.
4.   Schmitt Block Rooming House, 946 3rd Avenue where the Earp's stayed for a long period. The original building is long gone.
5. Wyatt Earp saloon and gambling hall, 951 4th Avenue, now a pawn shop .and jewelry store, located across the street from Horton Plaza. The Schmitt Block Rooming House could be viewed from Wyatt's place across the open plaza.
6. Wyatt Earp saloon/gambling hall, name unknown, NW corner of 6th and E Streets.
7. Louis Bank of Commerce, 837 5th Avenue where Wyatt operated the Oyster Bar (saloon/gambling hall/brothel). It has been reported that the owner of this building was a distant relative of Josie Earp. This was one of the best known and frequented busi-

nesses in the city. The upstairs lodging rooms were known as the Golden Poppy and were occupied by "ladies of the evening." Each room was painted a different color and each lady would wear a matching dress. How about that for innovation in the 1880s? This building was restored by noted architect Don Reeves and remains one of San Diego's finest examples of Victorian architecture.

8. Prostitution, Yuma Hotel, 631-635 5th Avenue. This "parlor house" has the distinction of being the first raided and closed by police in 1912. However, within a few days, they were back in business. The city fathers wanted to clean up the Red Light District before the opening of our 1915 Exposition in Balboa Park. They succeeded only in shifting the girls from the Gaslamp/Stingaree to other, more respectable areas of the city.

9. Wyatt Earp saloon/gambling hall located just south of the St. James Hotel. It is rumored that Wyatt ran the highest stakes faro game at this location. Little else is known.

10. Prostitution, Lincoln Hotel, 536 5th Avenue. This hotel operated at full speed until the early years of WW II, when the US Navy stepped in and closed all residential prostitution because of health considerations.

11. Prostitution, Brighton Rooms, SW corner of 5th and Market Streets. This was another favorite of servicemen.

12. Prostitution, Stingaree Hotel, 538-542 5th Avenue. This hotel was named for the old Stingaree District. The name was apt as many men were stung.

13. Prostitution, Fleet Hotel, 554 5th Avenue. This hotel catered to the entire Pacific Fleet during the early years of WW II.

14. Chinese Museum, NW corner of 3rd and J Streets. This beautiful museum opened in 1996 and features a lovely Chinese garden. This location was the center of a sizable Chinese Community in Wyatt's day.

15. Wyatt Earp residence, the famous Horton Grand Hotel, located between 3rd and 4th Streets on Island Avenue. This building was moved, brick by brick, to this location in recent years. Wyatt occupied room 104 for a considerable period of time. The hotel provides tours of this room during the summer's annual Wyatt

Earp Days celebration.

16. Prostitution, the infamous Canary House, operated by the best known of the Gaslamps/Stingaree's madams, Ida Bailey. The house was located in the rear of 536 4th Avenue, now the Gaslamp Quarter Hotel. Here it is rumored San Diego's elite gathered, including the Chief of Police and Mayor. Ida is famous for parading her "girls" all over San Diego's finest neighborhoods in a fine carriage. It is reported that good women pulled their shades when this colorful group passed by. The lower floor of the hotel in front is suspected of being a front for the Fan Tan gambling hall.

17. Prostitution, Anchor Hotel, 560 4th Avenue, the Anchor Hotel which occupied the rooms above the Royal Pie Bakery. The owner of the building has told the author that the Anchor Hotel was famous during WW II for its immorality and that servicemen would line up on the sidewalk around the block awaiting their turn. He stated that many years ago his sons and other bakery employees would stand on the sidewalk and flirt with the girls upstairs. One day he returned to the bakery and found his entire crew on the sidewalk talking to the girls, while two-hundred pies were burning to a crisp. Burning with anger, he immediately closed the hotel and the rooms were never again rented. At the turn of the century, part of this building was used as a Chinese gambling hall.

BIBLIOGRAPHY

Chapter 1

1.   Chaput, Don, *Virgil Earp, Western Peace Officer*, Affiliated Writers of America/Publishers, Encampment, Wyoming, 1994.
2.   Lake, Stuart N., *Wyatt Earp, Frontier Marshal*, Boston, 1931.
3.   Myers, John Myers, *Doc Holliday*, University of Nebraska Press, Lincoln, 1955.

Chapter 2

4.   Earp, Josephine Sarah Marcus, *I Married Wyatt Earp*, Recollections, Collected and Edited by Glenn G. Boyer, University of Arizona Press, Tucson, 1976.
5.   Erwin, Richard E., *The Truth About Wyatt Earp*, The O.K. Press, Carpinteria, 1993.
6.   *San Diego Union*, October 29, 1881.
7.   Chaput, Don, *Virgil Earp, Western Peace Officer,* Affiliated Writers of America/Publishers, Encampment, Wyoming, 1994.
8.   *San Diego Union*, March, 18 1881.
9.   *San Diego Union*, March 20, 1881.
10. *San Diego Union*, March 20, 1881.
11. *San Diego Union*, March 21, 1881.
12. *San Diego Union*, March 23, 1881.
13. Lake, Stuart, *Wyatt Earp, Frontier Marshal,* Boston, 1931.
14. Looney, Ralph, *Haunted Highways, The Ghost Towns of New Mexico,* University of New Mexico Press, Albuquerque, 1968.
15. Boyer, Glenn G., *Wyatt Earp's Tombstone Vendetta*, Talei, Honolulu. 1993.
16. Earp, Josephine Sarah Marcus, *I Married Wyatt Earp*, Recollections, Collected and Edited by Glenn G, Boyer, Univ, Arizona Press, 1976, p79.
17. *San Diego Union*, October 22, 1972.

Chapter 3

18. Earp, Josephine Sarah Marcus, *I Married Wyatt Earp*, Collected and Edited by Glenn G. Boyer, Univ. Arizona Press., 1976.
19. Erwin, Richard E., *The Truth About Wyatt Earp,* O.K. Press, 1993.
20. *Spokane Chronicle, Idaho Knew Wyatt Earp, Famed Lawman of the Old West Involved in Old Law Suits*, by Eldon Coroch, June 20, 1959.

Chapter 4

21. Lake, Stuart N., *Wyatt Earp, Frontier Marshal*, Boston, 1931.
22. Chaput, Don, *Virgil Earp, Western Peace Officer*, Affiliated Writers of America/Publishers, Encampment, Wyoming, 1994.
23. Lake, Stuart N., *Wyatt Earp, Frontier Marshal*, Boston, 1931.
24. MacMullen, G.F., one typewritten page addressed to the files, Sports-Boxing, *San Diego Union*, November 28, 1957
25. *San Diego City Directory*, 1887.
26. Earp, Jossehine Sarah Marcus, *I Married Wyatt Earp*, Recollections, Collected and Edited by Glenn G. Boyer, Univ, Arizona Press, 1976.
27. Interview with Judy, last name unknown, at Gaslamp Historical Museum, May 8, 1995.
28. Bachman, Curry Archie, Interview by Edgar F. Hastings, March 8, 1961, San Diego Historical Society, Oral History Program.
29. Fisher, Hugo Senator and Retired Superior Court Judge, Interview, Gaslamp Museum, August, 1996.
30. Reeves, Don, Architect and pioneer of Gaslamp Quarter restoration, Gaslamp Museum, October, 1996.
31. *San Diego Union*, October 17, 1978.
32. *San Diego Union*, October 17, 1978.
33. *San Diego Union*, October 17, 1978
34. Pearson, Adalaska, Old Time Law Enforcement Officer, typewritten reminiscences of an Old Timer, Ad Pearson, Mayor of Duckville, written about 1928, San Diego Historical Society.

35. *San Diego Union*, July 23, 1961.

Chapter 6

36. *San Diego Union*, February 1, 1894.
37. *San Diego Union*, April 15, 1908.
38. Glasscock, Carl Burgess, *Lucky Baldwin*, Indianapolis, Bobbs-Merrill, 1931.
39. Earp, Jospehine Sarah Marcus, *I Married Wyatt Earp*, Recollections, Collected and Edited by Glenn G. Boyer, Univ. of Arizona Press, 1976.
40. Interview with unknown Old Timer, Gaslamp Museum, Summer, 1996.
41. *San Diego Union*, dateline San Francisco, April 5, 1896.
42. *San Diego Union*, dateline San Francisco, April 5, 1896.
43. *San Diego Union*, dateline San Francisco, April 5, 1896.

Chapter 7

44. Service, Robert, *Ploughman of the Moon*, Dodd, Mead, New York, 1945.
45. Service, Robert, *The Spell of the Yukon*, Dodd, Mead, 1907.
46. Glasscock, G.B., *Lucky Baldwin,* Indianapolis, Bobbs-Merrill, 1933.
47. Beach, Rex, *The Spoilers,* New York, A. L. Burt Co., 1908.
48. Kearns, Doc, long time manager of heavyweight champion Jack Dempsey, a series of interviews along with Johnny "Spaghetti Joe" Keyes and Bob Johnston, owner of the Palace Bar and Hollywood Burlesque Theatre.
49. *Record Breaking Run of the Scott Special, Los Angeles to Chicago*, Santa Fe Railroad, illus., no date.
50. *San Diego Union*, March 25, 1906.

Chapter 8

51. *San Diego Union*, dateline Los Angeles, date unknown.

52. *Needles Desert Star*, July 6, 1988.

Chapter 9

53. Hutton, Paul A., magazine article, "*Celluloid Lawman*, or *Wyatt Earp Goes to Hollywood*, Montana, The Magazine of Western History, Summer, 1995.
54. Wallechinsky, David and Irving Wallace, *The People's Almanac, #2*, Morrow, New York, 1978, p 526.
55. Lake, Stuart N., *Wyatt Earp, Frontier Marshal,* Boston, 1931.

Chapter 10

56. *San Diego Union*, January 28, 1964.
57. *San Diego Union,* October 30, 1960.
58. Lake, Stuart N., Interview by the San Diego Historical Society, Oral History Program, Date and interviewer unknown.
59. Lake, Stuart N., *Wyatt Earp, Frontier Marshal*, Boston, 1931.
60. Hutton, Paul A., magazine article, *Celluloid Lawman* or *Wyatt Earp Goes to Hollywood*, Montana, *Magazine of Western History*, Summer, 1995.
61. Lake, Stuart N., *Wyatt Earp, Frontier Marshal*, Boston, 1931.

Chapter 11

62. *San Diego Union*, dateline Los Angeles, January 17, 1929.
63. Earp, Jospehine Marcus, *I Married Wyatt Earp, Recollections,* Collected and Edited by Glenn G. Boyer, Univ. of Arizona Press, 1976.

Chapter 12

64. Weddle, Henry H., three interviews by Edgar F. Hastings, Feb. 25, Aug. 20, Dec. 30, 1959, San Diego Historical Society, Oral History Program.

65. *San Diego Union*, column by Don Freeman, October 2, 1972.
66. *San Diego Union* newspaper article, date unknown.
67. Dodge, Fred, *Undercover for Wells Fargo, The Unvarnished Recollections Of,* Edited by Carolyn Lake, Boston, Houghton, Mifflin, 1969.
68. *Boerne Texas Star,* Fred Dodge obituary, November 22, 1938.
69. Erwin, Richard E., *The Truth About Wyatt Earp,* O.K. Press, 1993.

Epilogue

70. Twain, Mark, *Roughing It,* Hartford, American Pub. Co., 1872.